Today I am grateful for...........

_____
_____
_____
_____
_____
_____
_____
_____
_____
_____

One awesome thing that
happened today was.......

_____
_____
_____
_____
_____
_____
_____

**MY HAPPINESS SCALE**

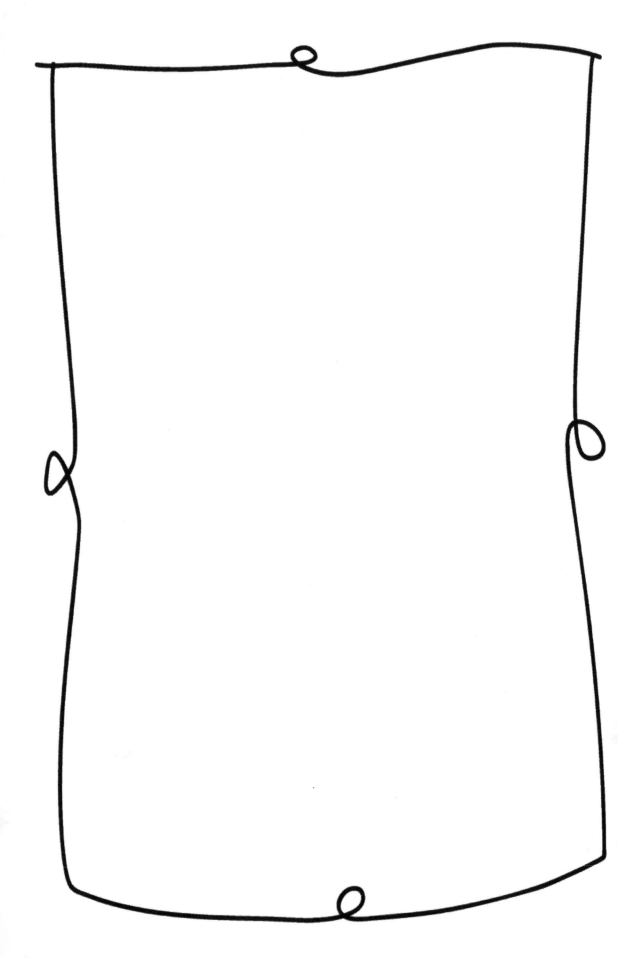

Today I am grateful for...........

One awesome thing that
happened today was.......

**MY
HAPPINESS
SCALE**

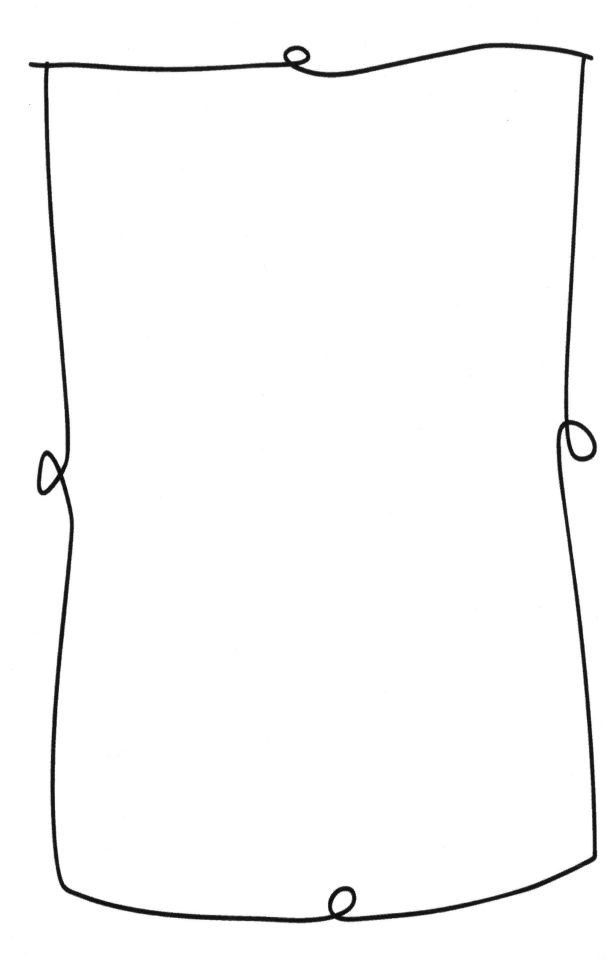

Today I am grateful for..........
_____
_____
_____
_____
_____
_____
_____
_____

One awesome thing that
happened today was.......
_____
_____
_____
_____
_____
_____

**MY
HAPPINESS
SCALE**

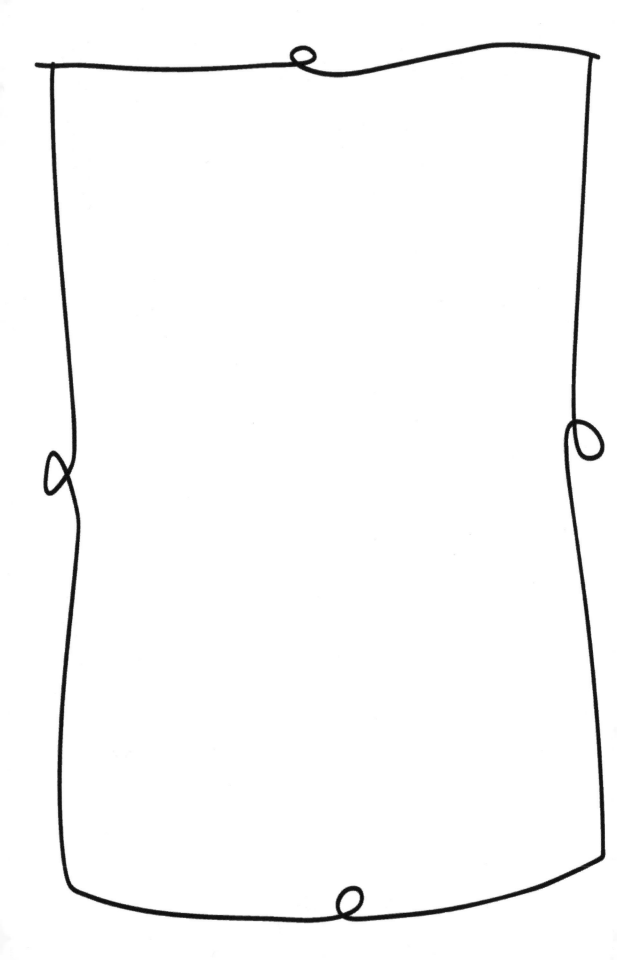

Today I am grateful for...........

One awesome thing that
happened today was.......

**MY
HAPPINESS
SCALE**

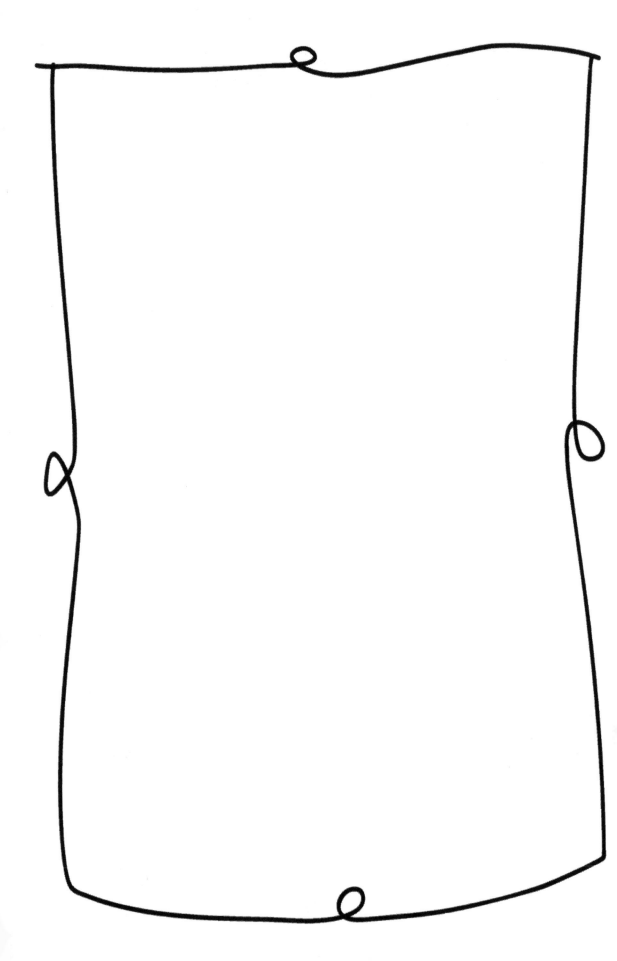

Today I am grateful for..........

_____
_____
_____
_____
_____
_____
_____
_____
_____
_____
_____
_____

One awesome thing that
happened today was.......

_____
_____
_____
_____
_____
_____
_____
_____

**MY
HAPPINESS
SCALE**

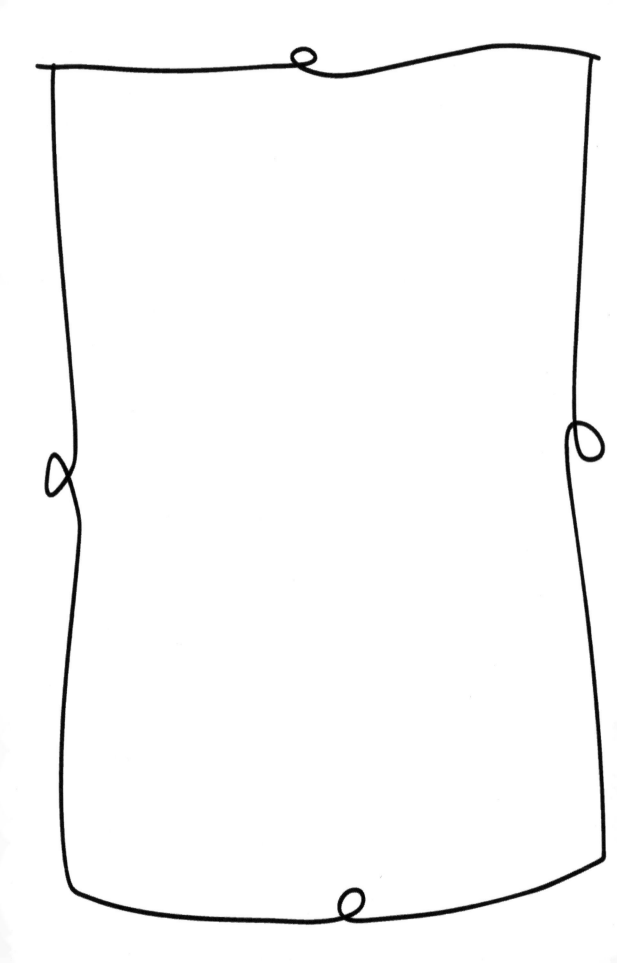

Today I am grateful for...........

_____
_____
_____
_____
_____
_____
_____
_____
_____
_____

One awesome thing that
happened today was.......

_____
_____
_____
_____
_____
_____
_____

**MY**
**HAPPINESS**
**SCALE**

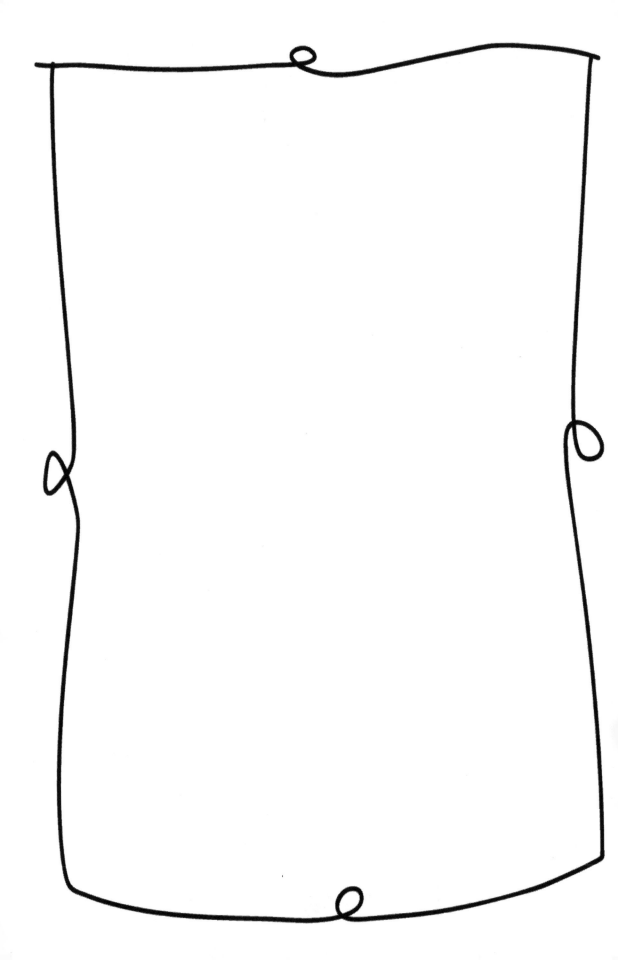

Today I am grateful for...........

_____
_____
_____
_____
_____
_____
_____
_____
_____
_____
_____

One awesome thing that
happened today was.......

_____
_____
_____
_____
_____
_____
_____
_____

**MY**
**HAPPINESS**
**SCALE**

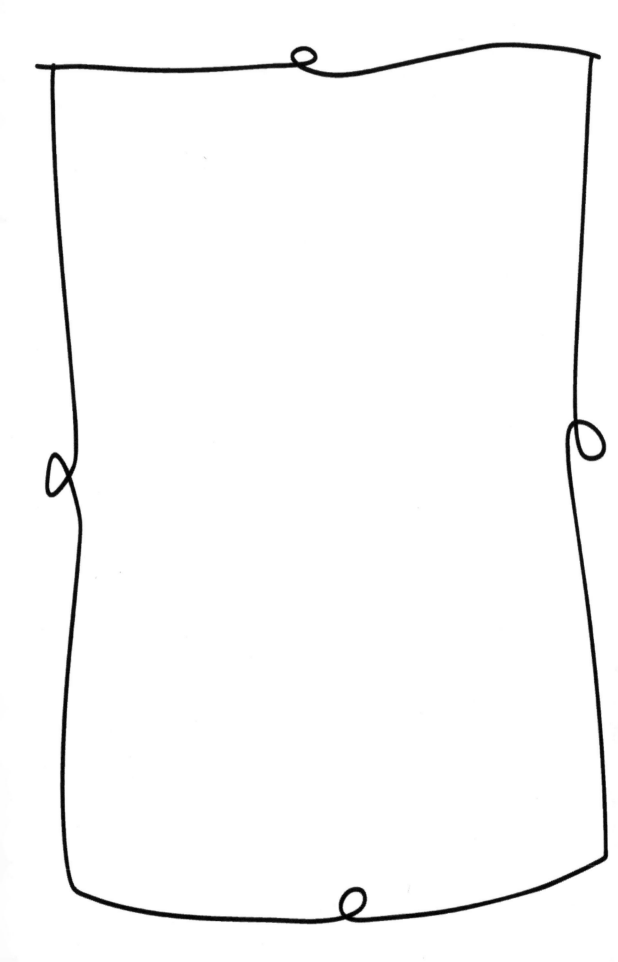

Today I am grateful for..........

_____
_____
_____
_____
_____
_____
_____
_____
_____
_____

One awesome thing that
happened today was.......

_____
_____
_____
_____
_____
_____
_____

**MY
HAPPINESS
SCALE**

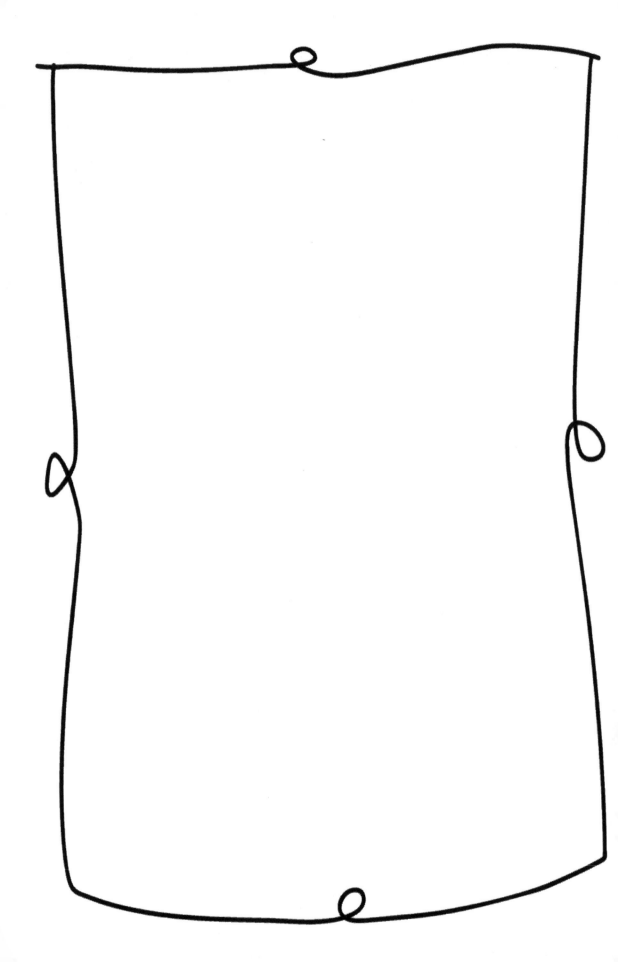

Today I am grateful for...........

_____
_____
_____
_____
_____
_____
_____
_____

One awesome thing that
happened today was.......

_____
_____
_____
_____
_____
_____

**MY
HAPPINESS
SCALE**

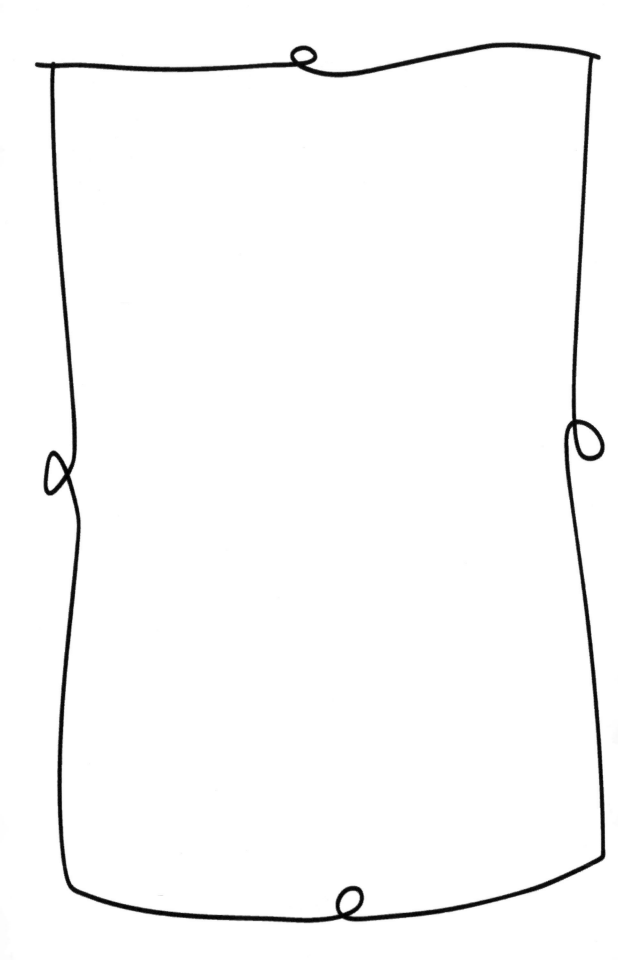

Today I am grateful for...........

_____
_____
_____
_____
_____
_____
_____
_____
_____
_____

One awesome thing that
happened today was.......

_____
_____
_____
_____
_____
_____
_____

**MY
HAPPINESS
SCALE**

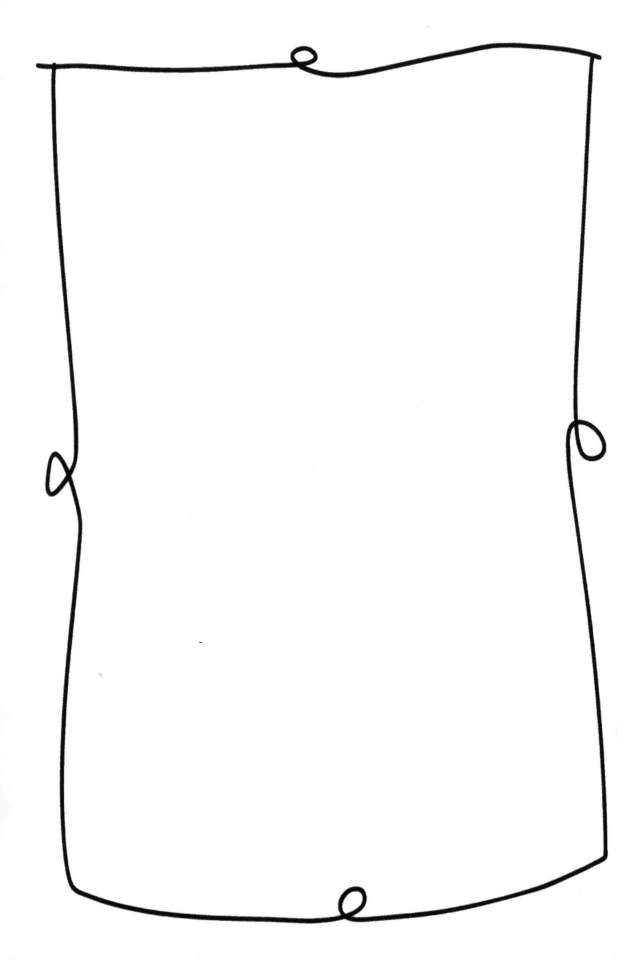

Today I am grateful for...........

One awesome thing that
happened today was.......

**MY
HAPPINESS
SCALE**

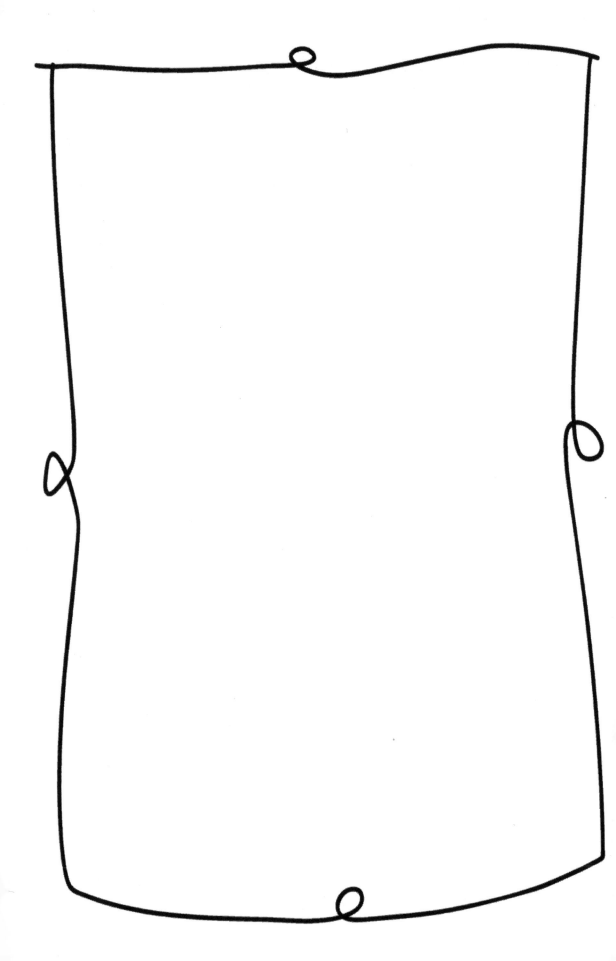

Today I am grateful for...........

One awesome thing that
happened today was.......

**MY HAPPINESS SCALE**

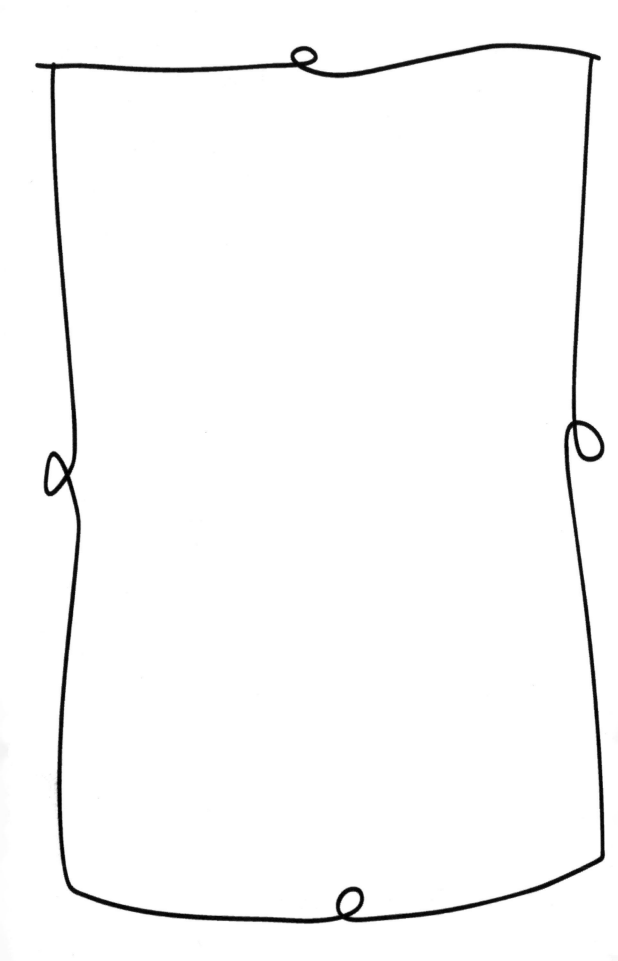

Today I am grateful for...........
_____
_____
_____
_____
_____
_____
_____
_____
_____
_____
_____

One awesome thing that
happened today was.......
_____
_____
_____
_____
_____
_____
_____
_____

**MY
HAPPINESS
SCALE**

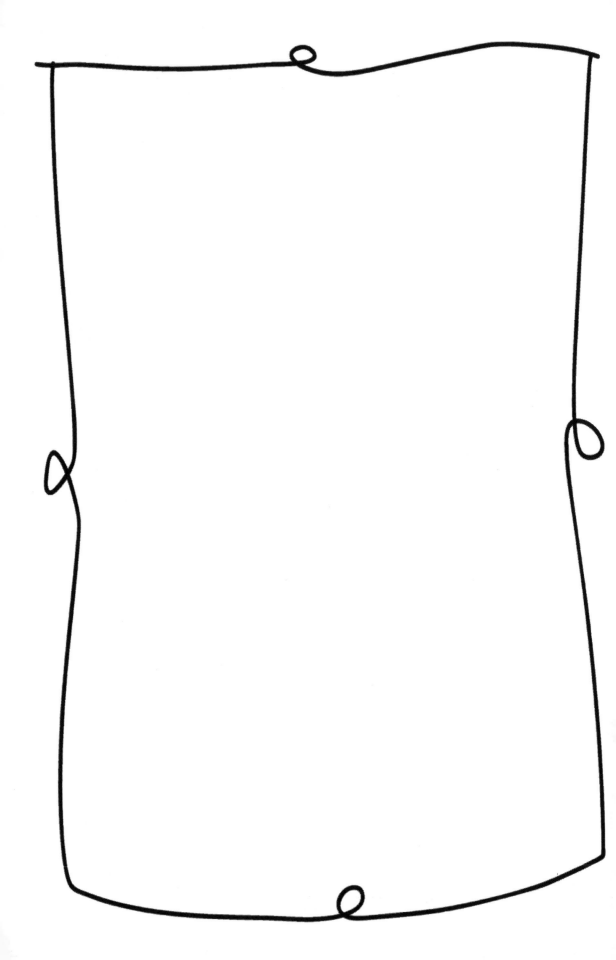

Today I am grateful for...........

_____
_____
_____
_____
_____
_____
_____
_____
_____
_____

One awesome thing that
happened today was.......

_____
_____
_____
_____
_____
_____
_____

**MY HAPPINESS SCALE**

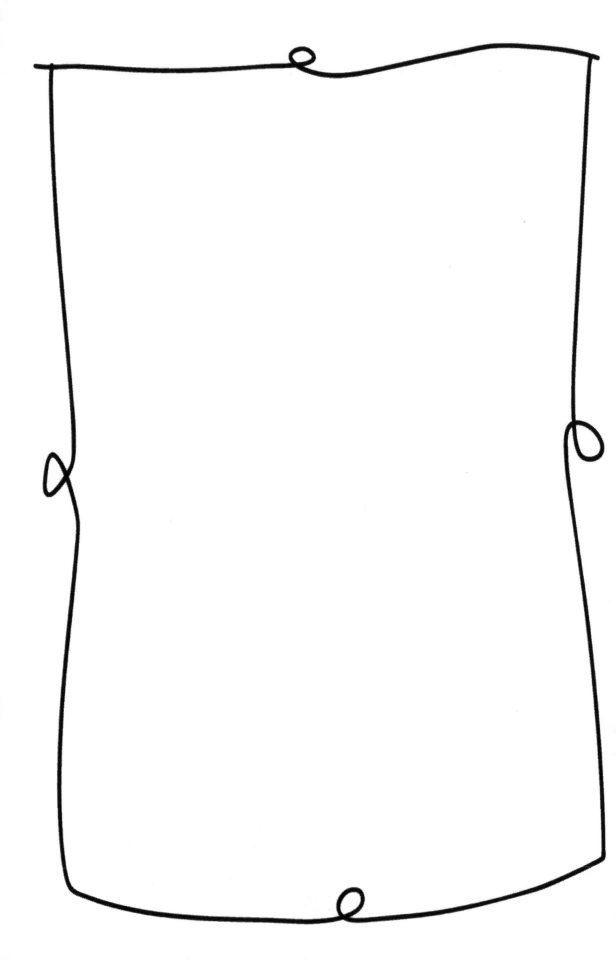

Today I am grateful for...........

_____
_____
_____
_____
_____
_____
_____
_____
_____
_____

One awesome thing that
happened today was.......
_____
_____
_____
_____
_____
_____
_____
_____

**MY
HAPPINESS
SCALE**

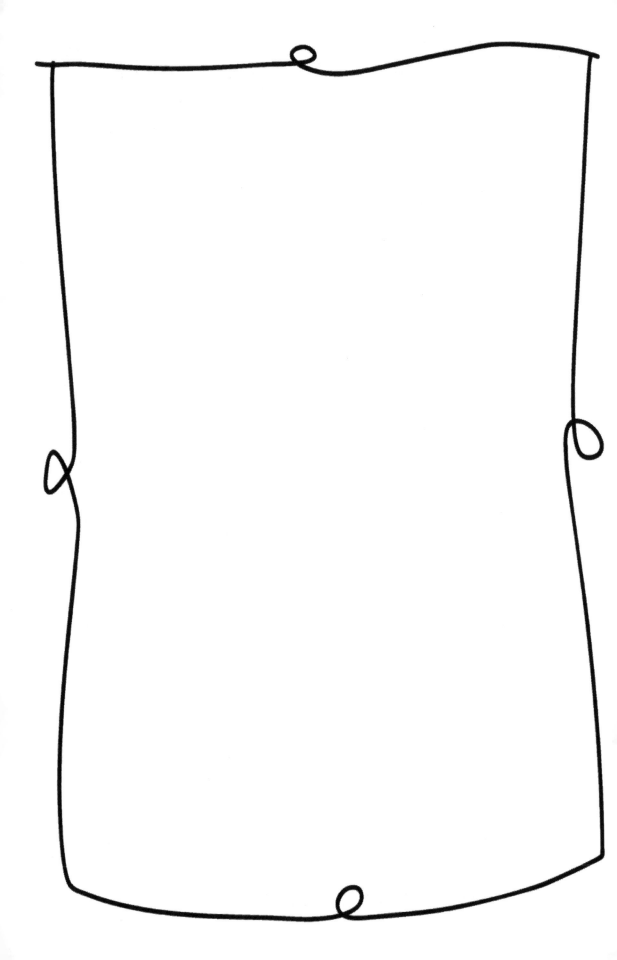

Today I am grateful for..........

One awesome thing that
happened today was.......

**MY
HAPPINESS
SCALE**

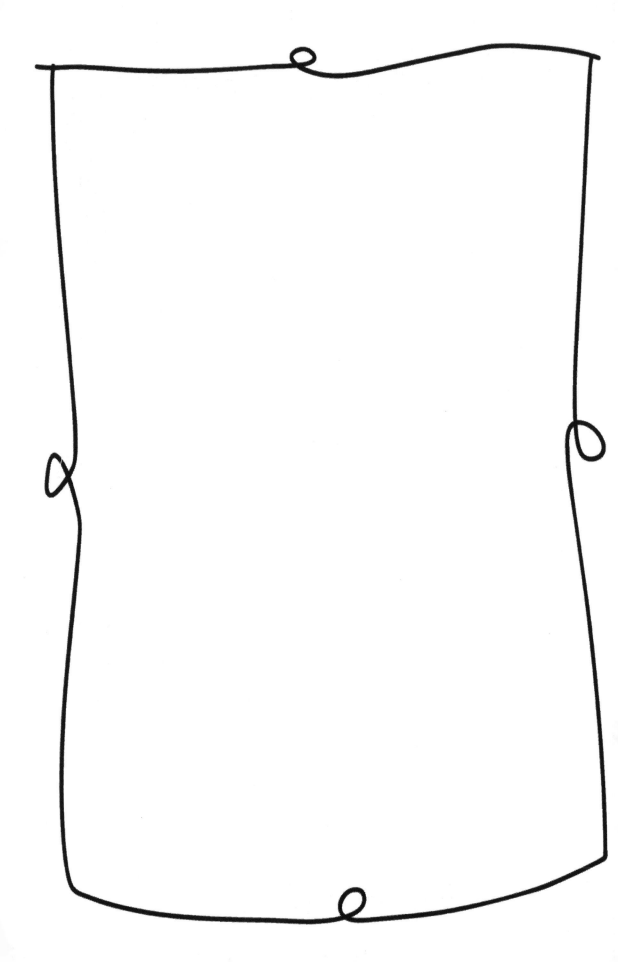

Today I am grateful for...........

One awesome thing that
happened today was.......

**MY**
**HAPPINESS**
**SCALE**

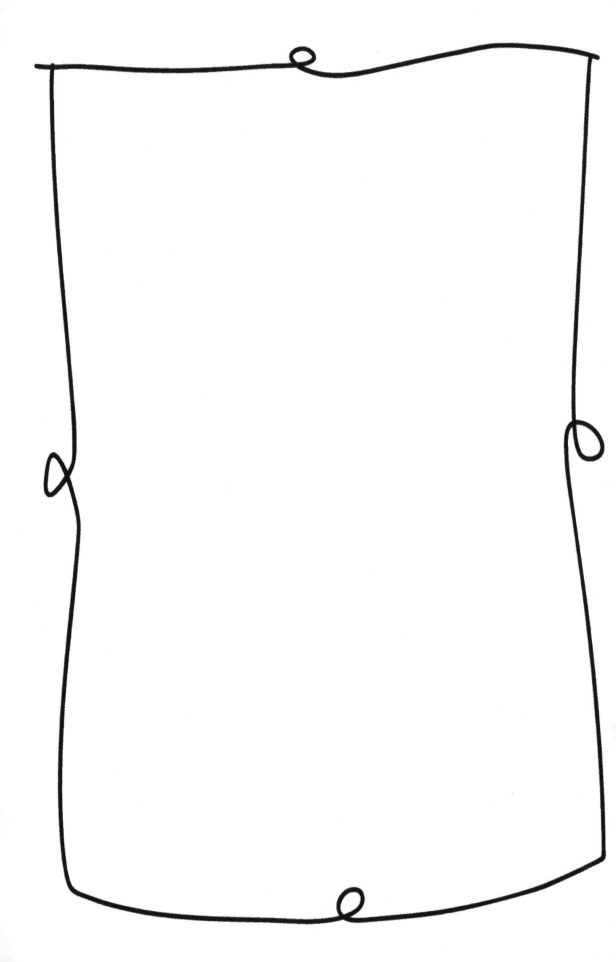

Today I am grateful for...........

_____
_____
_____
_____
_____
_____
_____
_____
_____
_____
_____

One awesome thing that
happened today was.......

_____
_____
_____
_____
_____
_____
_____
_____

**MY HAPPINESS SCALE**

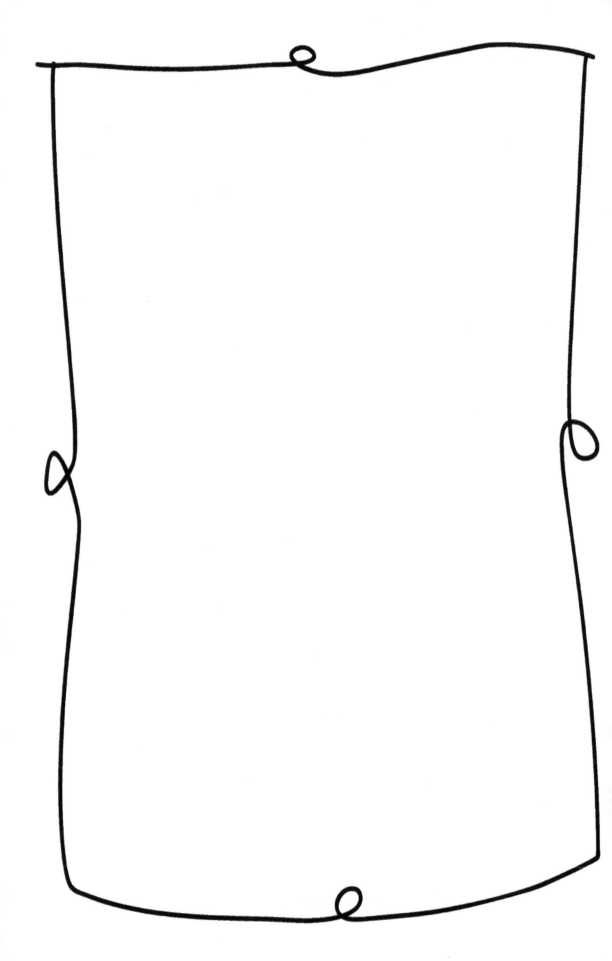

Today I am grateful for...........

_____
_____
_____
_____
_____
_____
_____
_____
_____
_____

One awesome thing that
happened today was.......

_____
_____
_____
_____
_____
_____

**MY HAPPINESS SCALE**

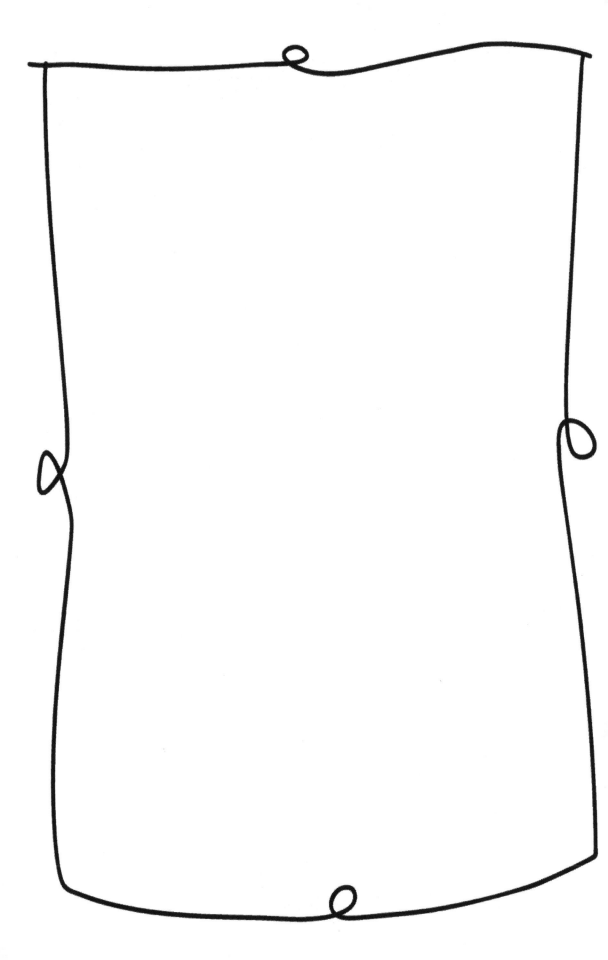

Today I am grateful for...........

One awesome thing that
happened today was......

**MY**
**HAPPINESS**
**SCALE**

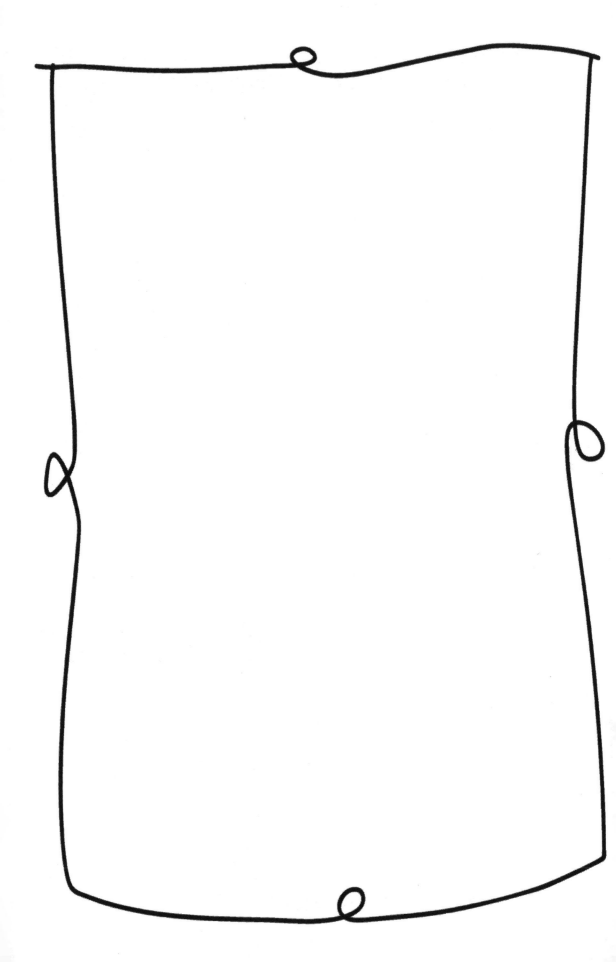

Today I am grateful for...........

One awesome thing that
happened today was.......

**MY
HAPPINESS
SCALE**

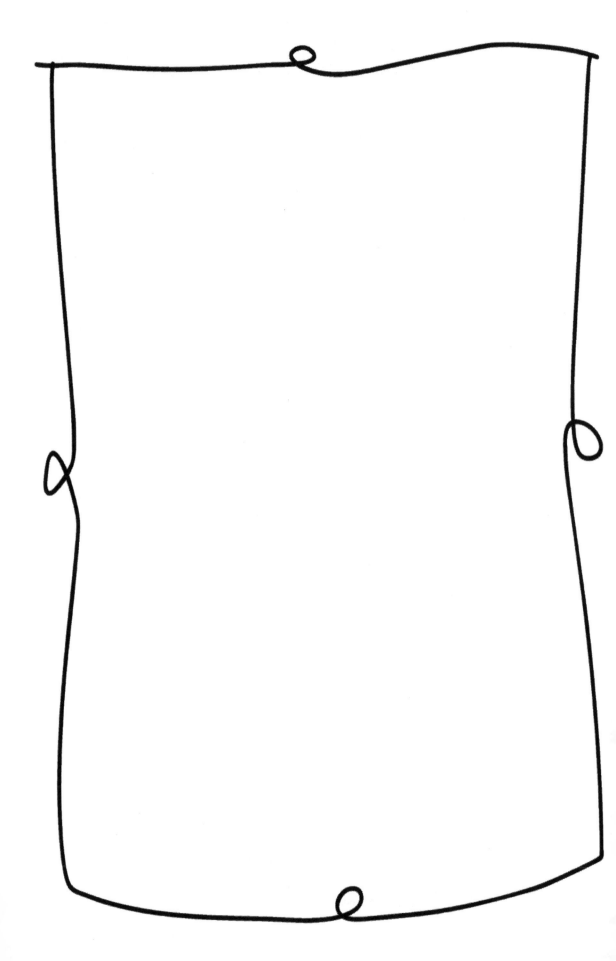

Today I am grateful for...........

_____
_____
_____
_____
_____
_____
_____
_____
_____
_____
_____

One awesome thing that
happened today was.......

_____
_____
_____
_____
_____
_____
_____

**MY HAPPINESS SCALE**

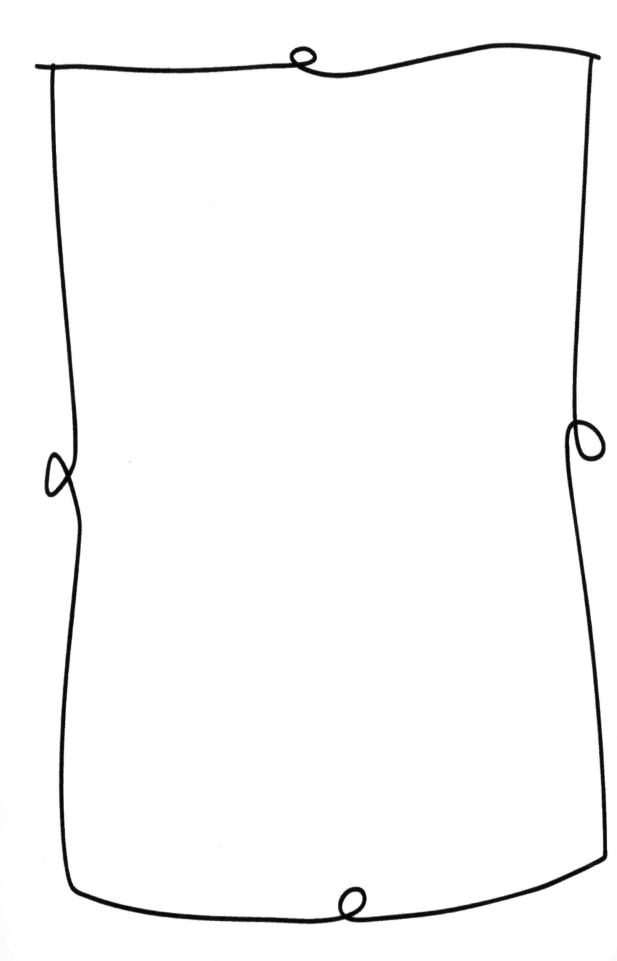

Today I am grateful for...........

One awesome thing that happened today was.......

**MY HAPPINESS SCALE**

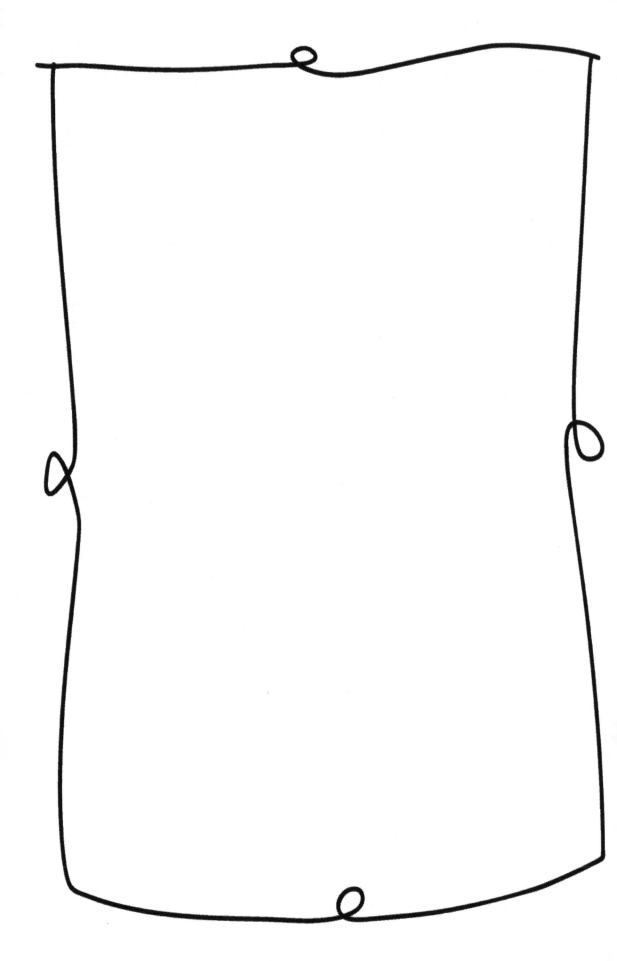

Today I am grateful for...........

_____
_____
_____
_____
_____
_____
_____
_____
_____
_____
_____

One awesome thing that
happened today was.......

_____
_____
_____
_____
_____
_____
_____
_____

**MY**
**HAPPINESS**
**SCALE**

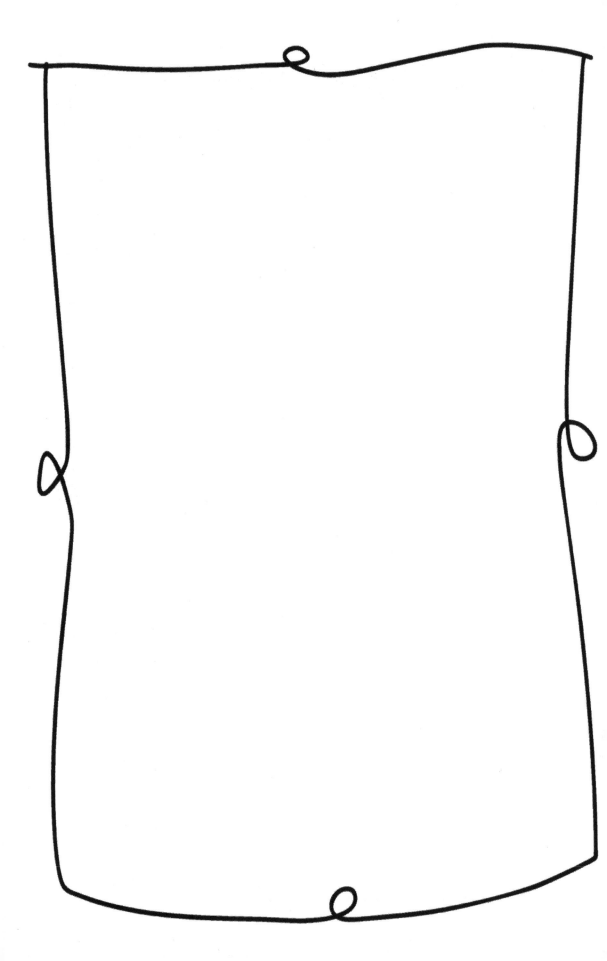

Today I am grateful for..........

One awesome thing that
happened today was.......

**MY**
**HAPPINESS**
**SCALE**

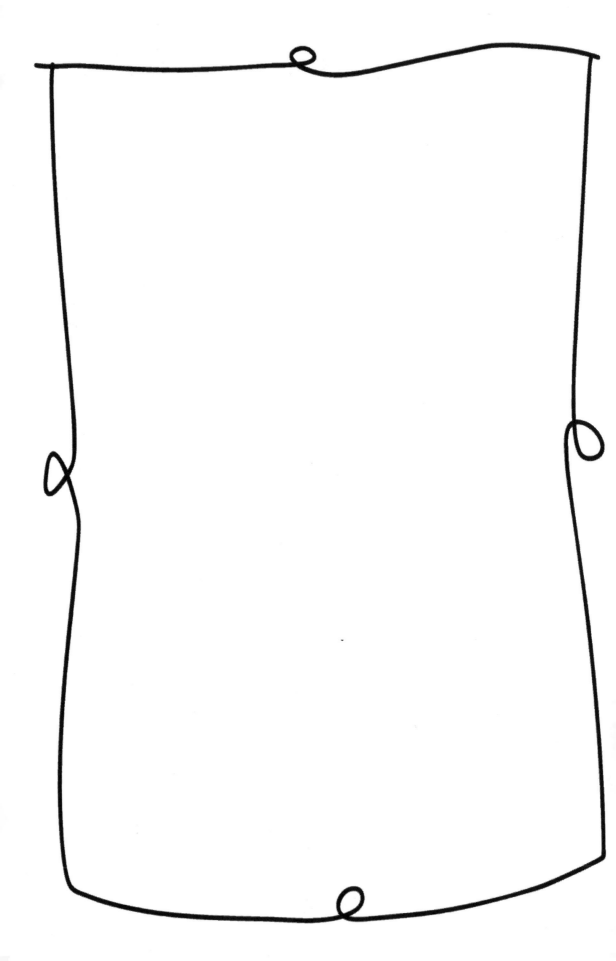

Today I am grateful for...........

_____
_____
_____
_____
_____
_____
_____
_____
_____
_____
_____
_____
_____

One awesome thing that
happened today was.......

_____
_____
_____
_____
_____
_____
_____

**MY
HAPPINESS
SCALE**

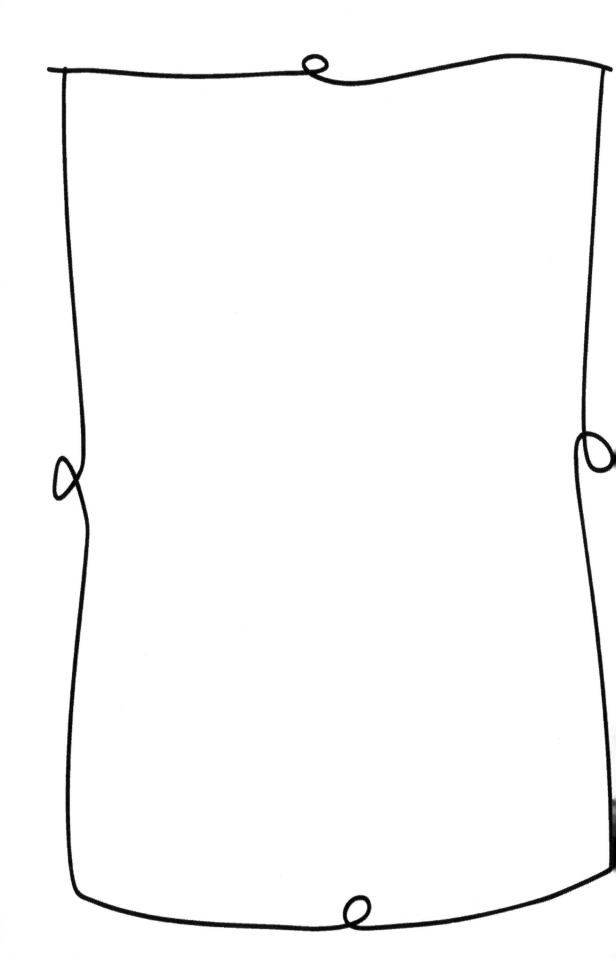

Today I am grateful for...........

One awesome thing that
happened today was.......

**MY HAPPINESS SCALE**

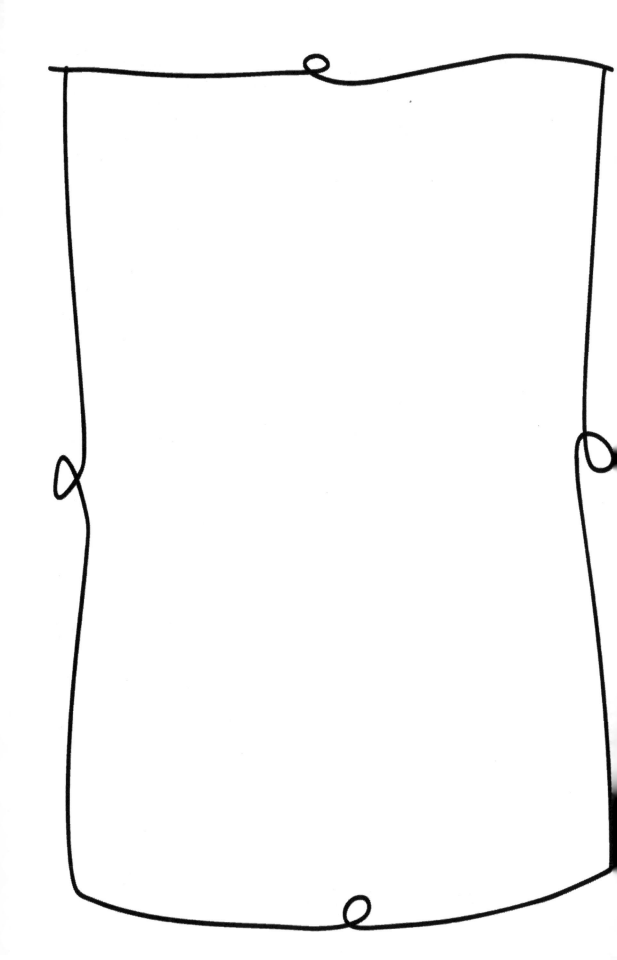

Today I am grateful for...........

_____
_____
_____
_____
_____
_____
_____
_____
_____
_____
_____
_____

One awesome thing that
happened today was.......

_____
_____
_____
_____
_____
_____
_____

**MY
HAPPINESS
SCALE**

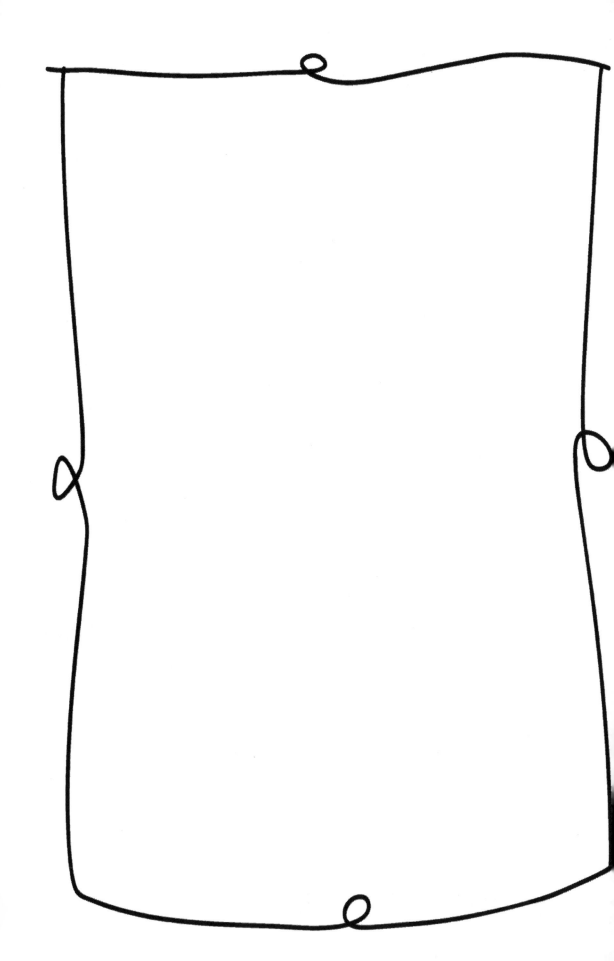

Today I am grateful for...........

One awesome thing that
happened today was.......

**MY
HAPPINESS
SCALE**

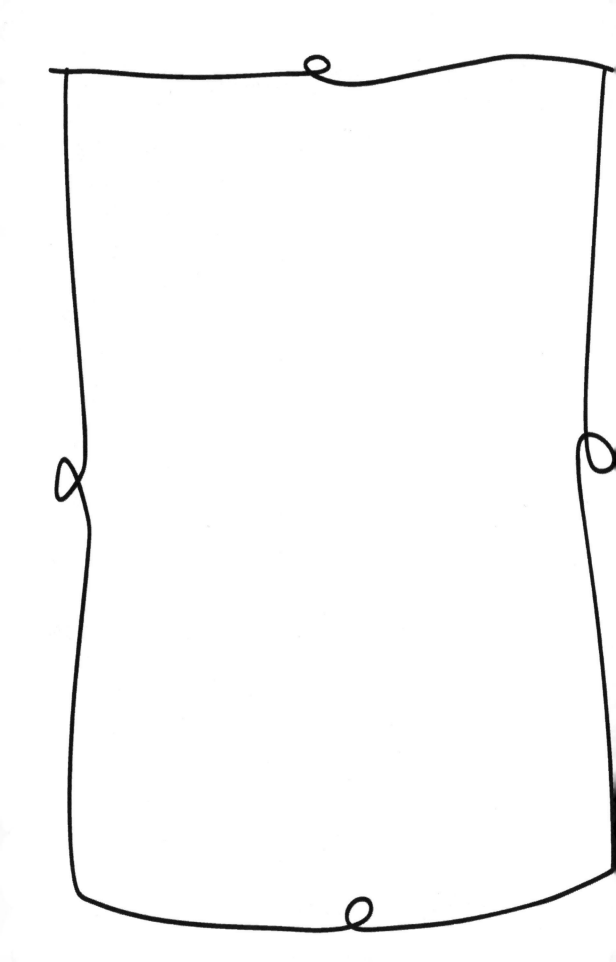

Today I am grateful for...........

One awesome thing that
happened today was.......

**MY HAPPINESS SCALE**

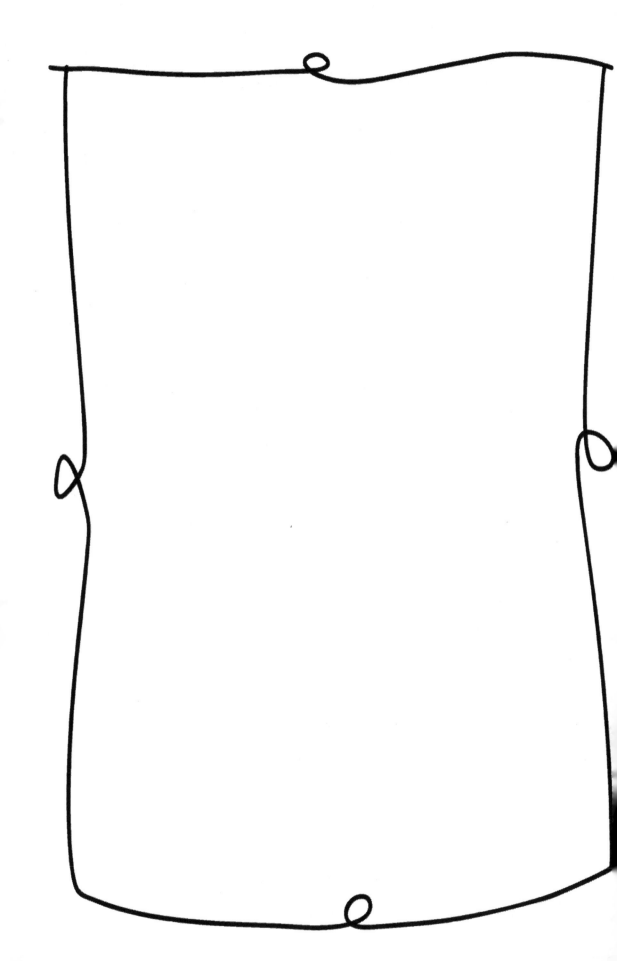

Today I am grateful for...........

One awesome thing that
happened today was.......

**MY**
**HAPPINESS**
**SCALE**

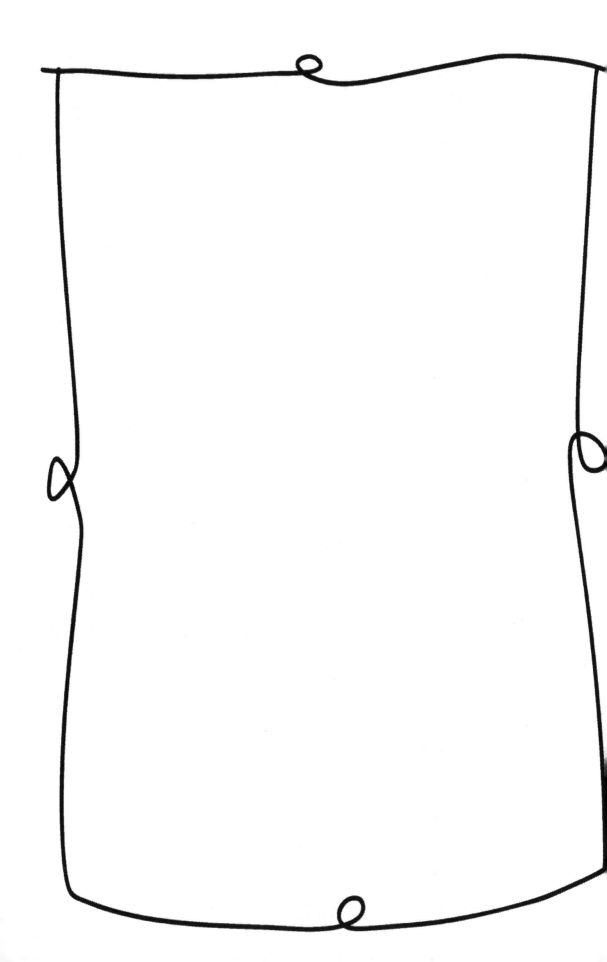

Today I am grateful for...........

_____

One awesome thing that
happened today was.......

**MY
HAPPINESS
SCALE**

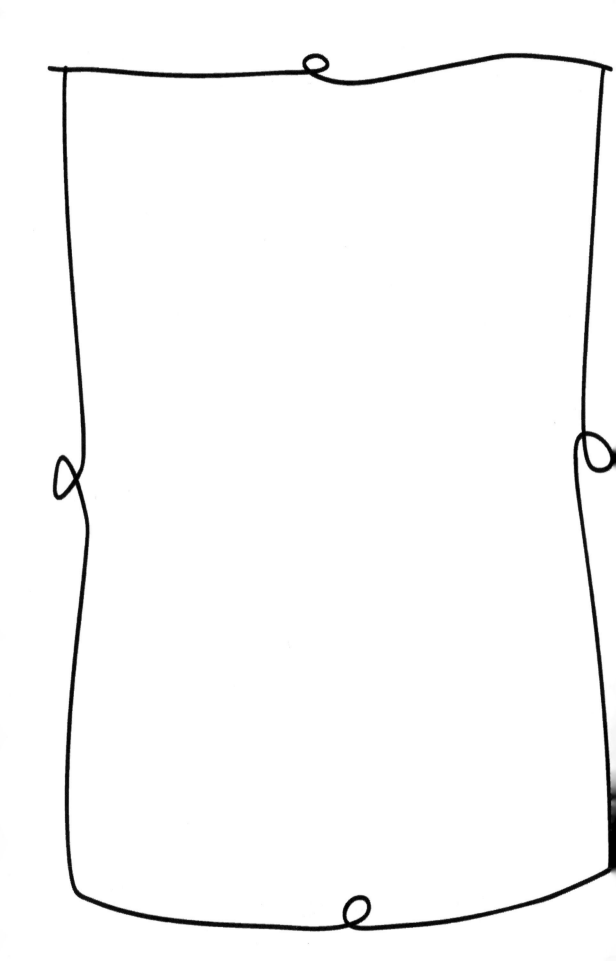

Today I am grateful for...........

_____
_____
_____
_____
_____
_____
_____
_____
_____
_____
_____
_____

One awesome thing that
happened today was.......

_____
_____
_____
_____
_____
_____
_____

**MY HAPPINESS SCALE**

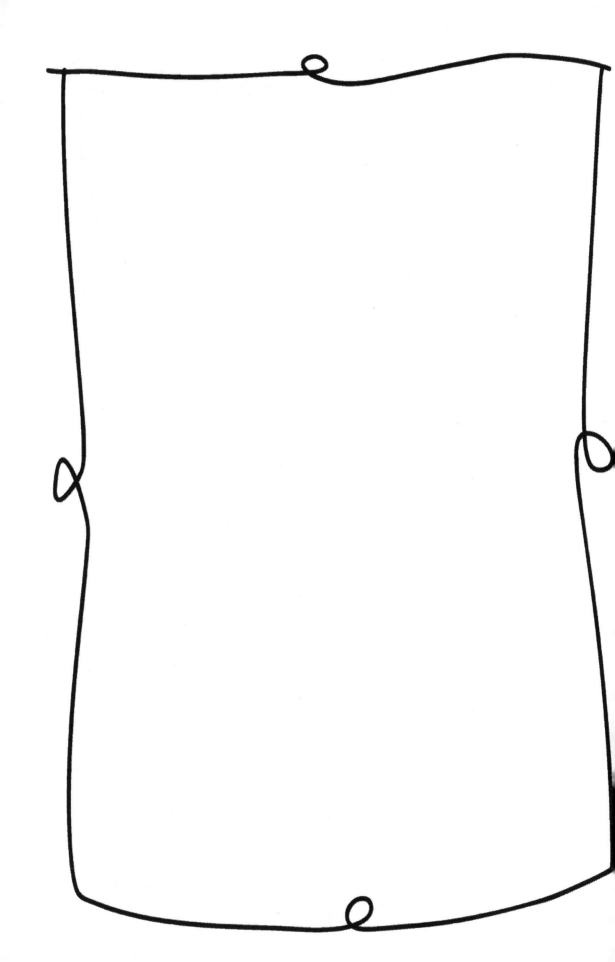

Today I am grateful for...........

_____
_____
_____
_____
_____
_____
_____
_____
_____
_____
_____
_____

One awesome thing that
happened today was.......

_____
_____
_____
_____
_____
_____
_____
_____
_____

**MY HAPPINESS SCALE**

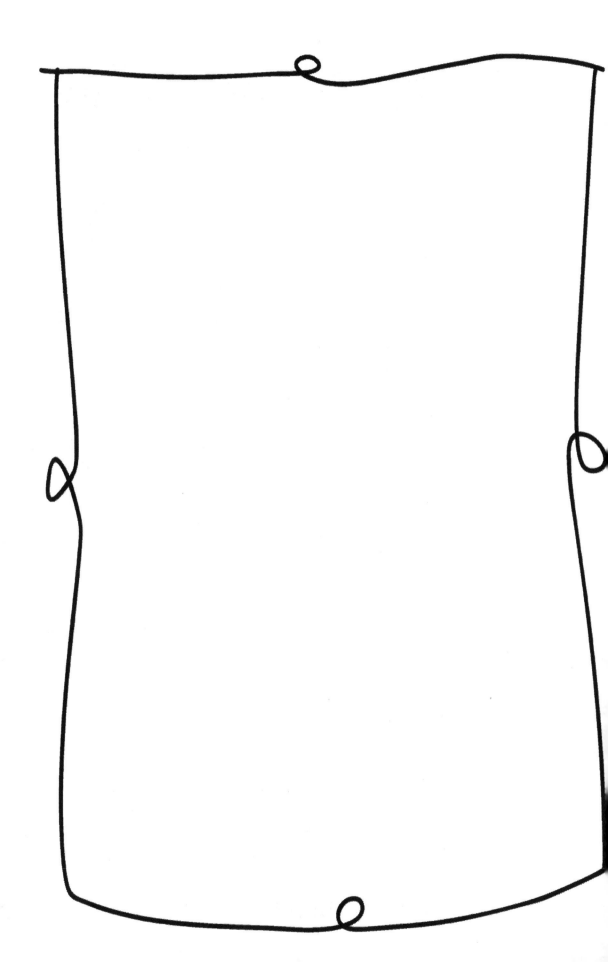

Today I am grateful for..........
_____
_____
_____
_____
_____
_____
_____
_____
_____
_____

One awesome thing that
happened today was.......
_____
_____
_____
_____
_____
_____
_____

**MY**
**HAPPINESS**
**SCALE**

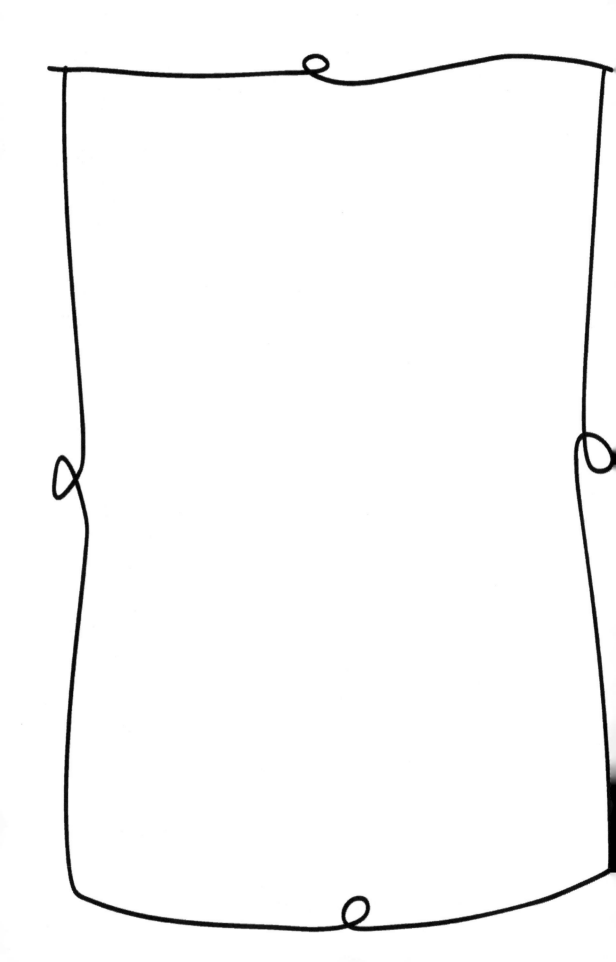

Today I am grateful for...........

One awesome thing that
happened today was.......

**MY**
**HAPPINESS**
**SCALE**

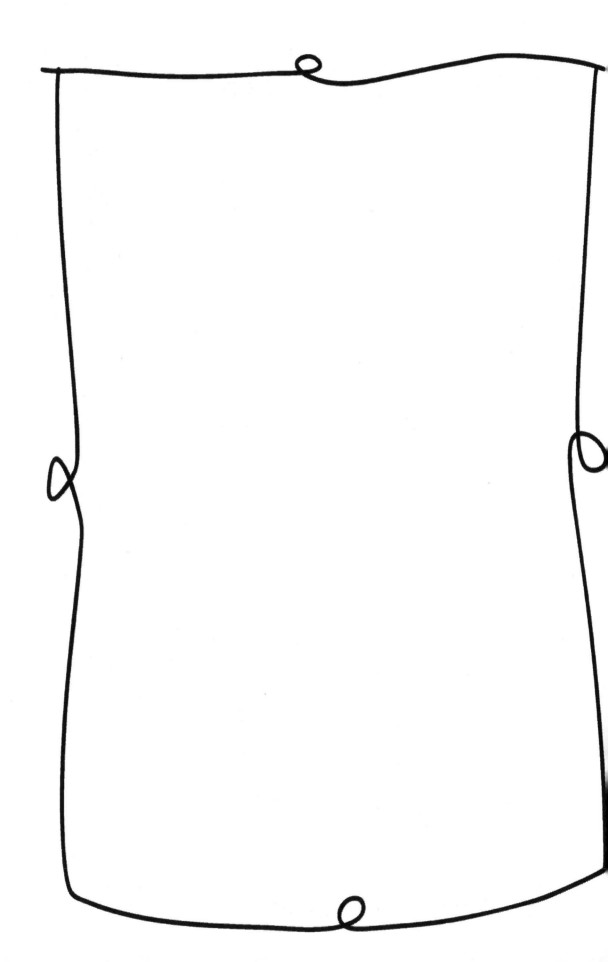

Today I am grateful for...........

One awesome thing that
happened today was.......

**MY**
**HAPPINESS**
**SCALE**

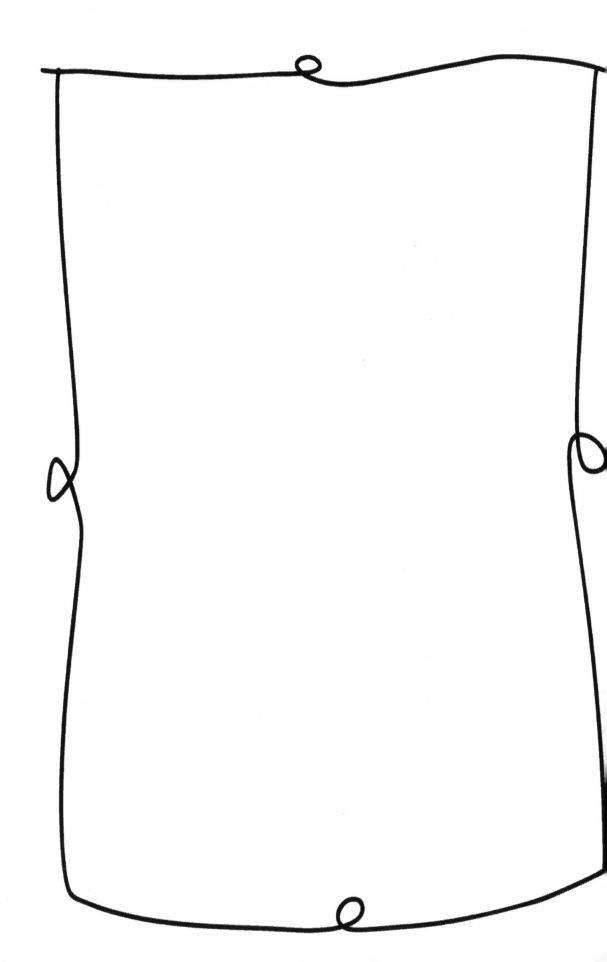

Today I am grateful for............

_____
_____
_____
_____
_____
_____
_____
_____
_____
_____
_____
_____
_____
_____

One awesome thing that
happened today was.......

_____
_____
_____
_____
_____
_____
_____
_____

**MY HAPPINESS SCALE**

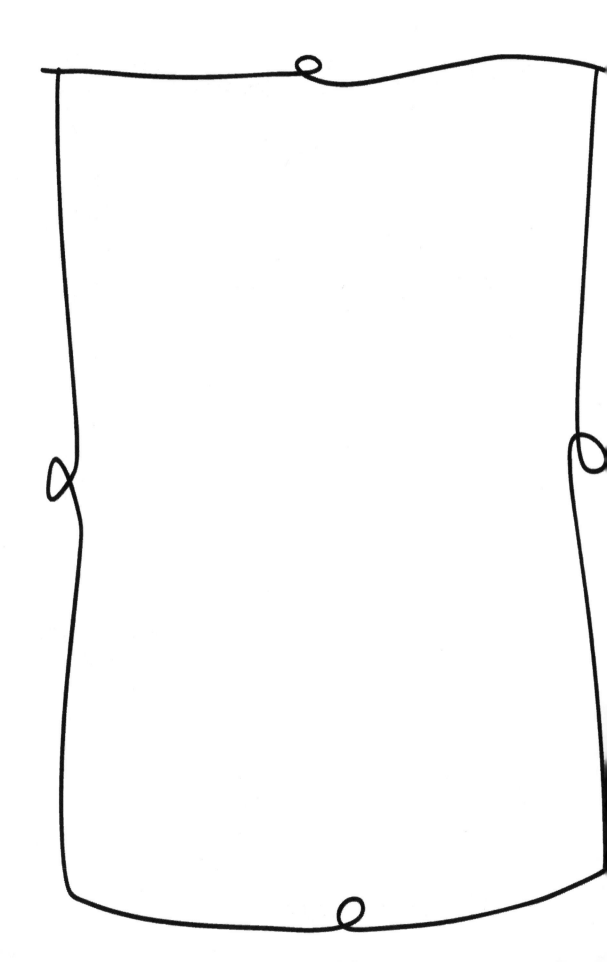

Today I am grateful for...........

_____
_____
_____
_____
_____
_____
_____
_____
_____
_____
_____
_____

One awesome thing that
happened today was.......

_____
_____
_____
_____
_____
_____
_____
_____
_____
_____

**MY
HAPPINESS
SCALE**

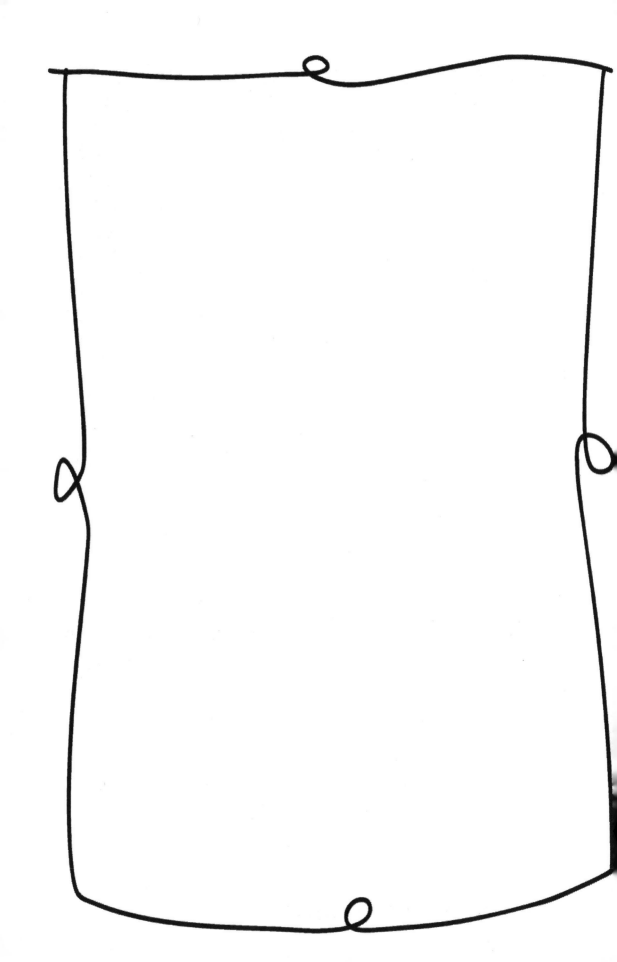

Today I am grateful for...........

One awesome thing that
happened today was.......

**MY HAPPINESS SCALE**

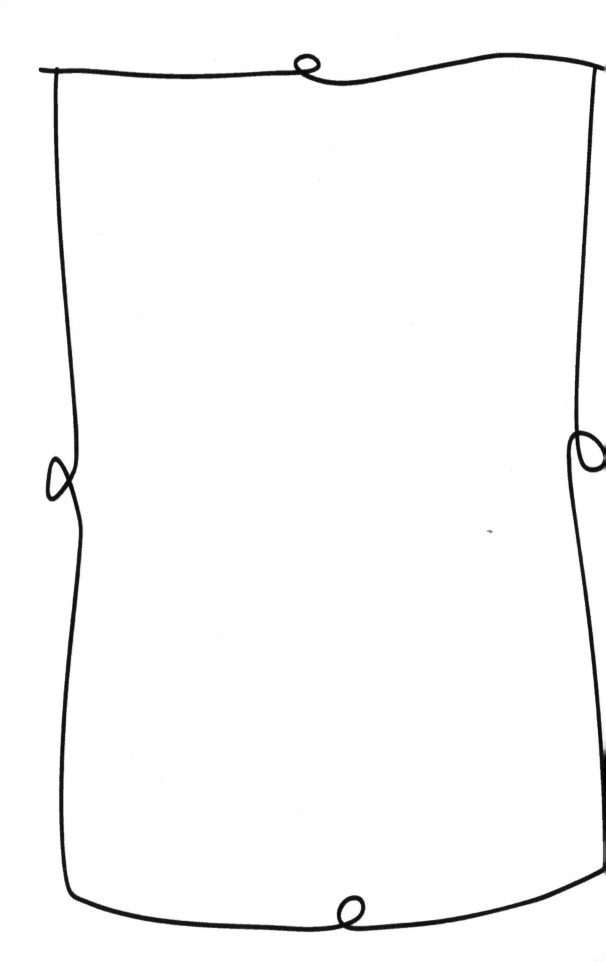

Today I am grateful for.............
_____
_____
_____
_____
_____
_____
_____
_____
_____
_____
_____
_____
_____

One awesome thing that
happened today was.......
_____
_____
_____
_____
_____
_____
_____
_____

**MY**
**HAPPINESS**
**SCALE**

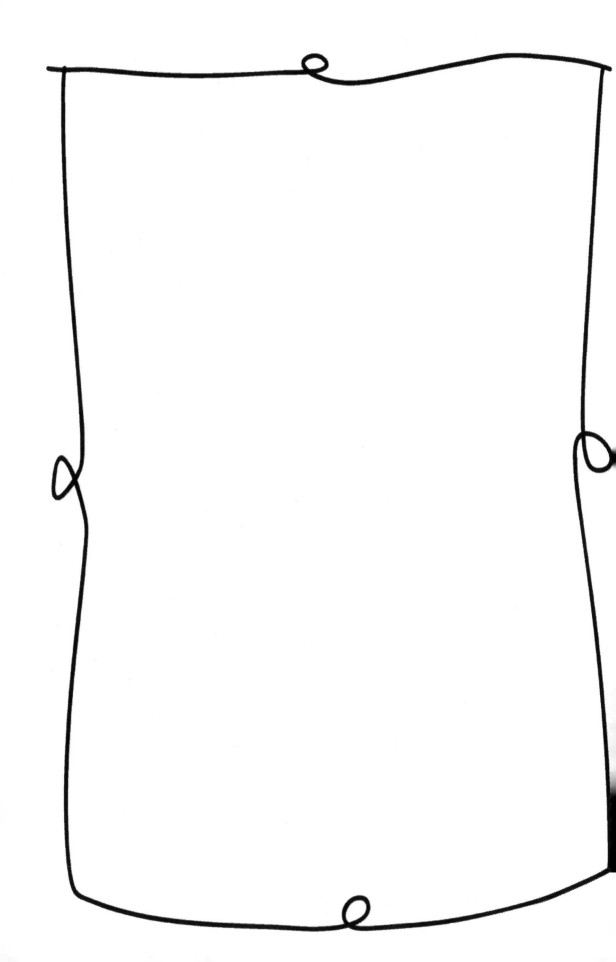

Today I am grateful for...........

One awesome thing that happened today was.......

**MY**
**HAPPINESS**
**SCALE**

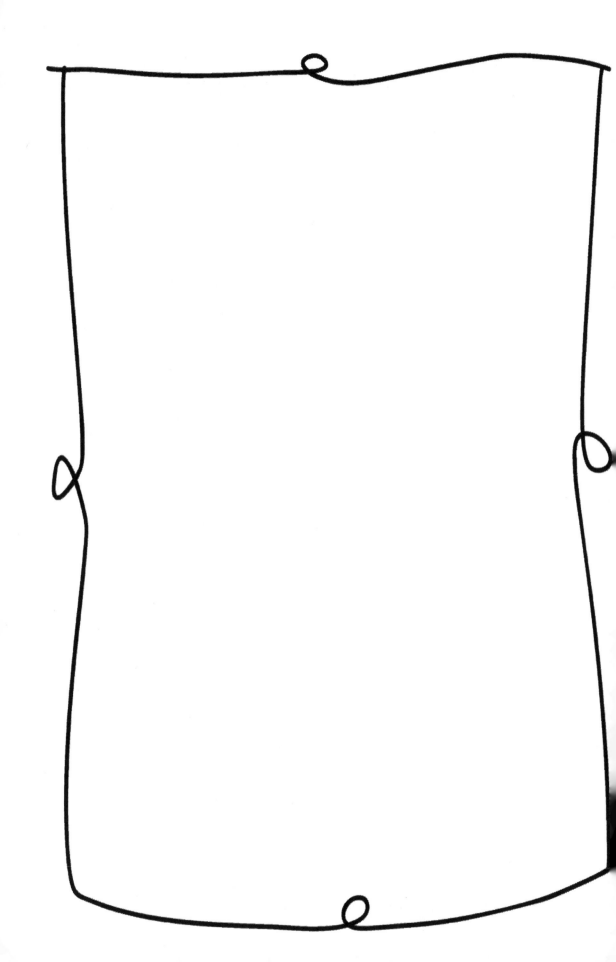

## Today I am grateful for..........

## One awesome thing that happened today was.......

**MY HAPPINESS SCALE**

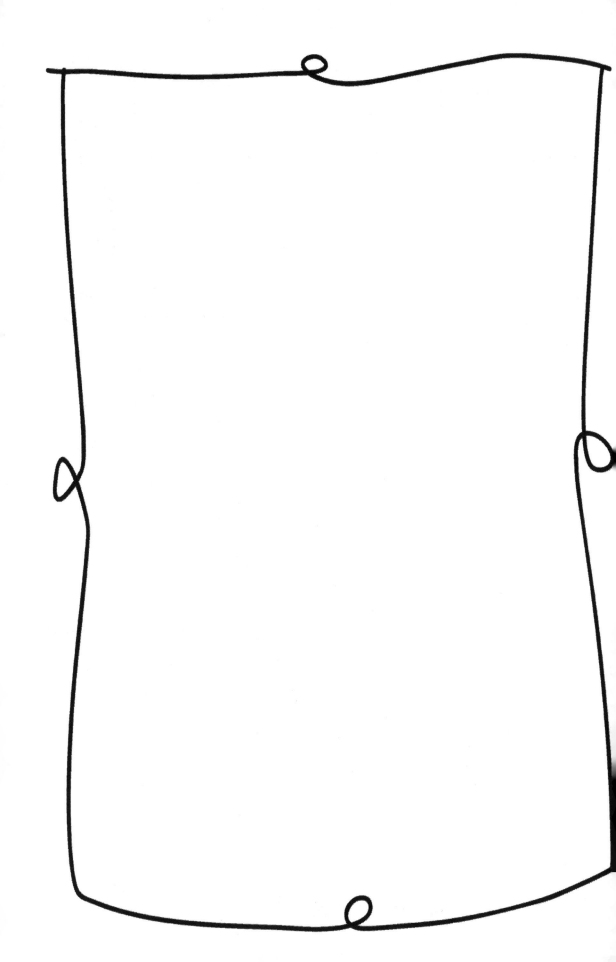

Today I am grateful for..........

_____
_____
_____
_____
_____
_____
_____
_____
_____
_____
_____
_____

One awesome thing that
happened today was.......

_____
_____
_____
_____
_____
_____
_____

**MY
HAPPINESS
SCALE**

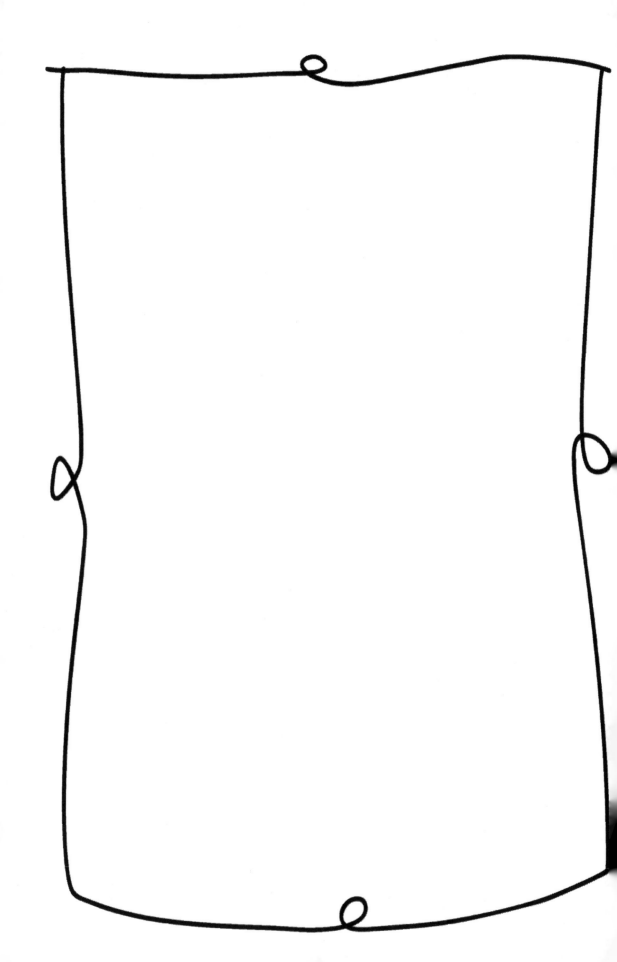

Today I am grateful for...........

_____
_____
_____
_____
_____
_____
_____
_____
_____
_____
_____

One awesome thing that
happened today was.......

_____
_____
_____
_____
_____
_____

**MY HAPPINESS SCALE**

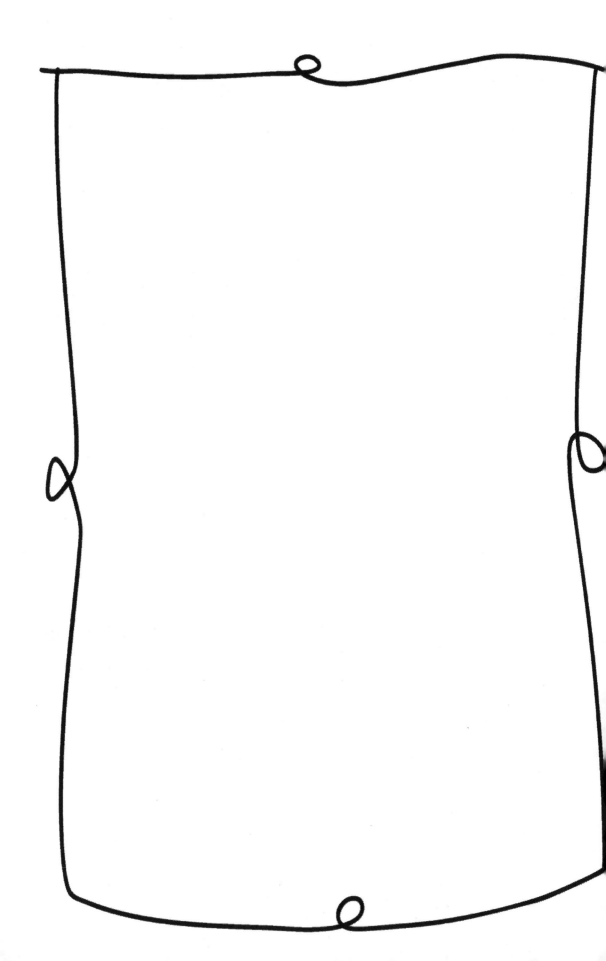

Today I am grateful for...........
_____
_____
_____
_____
_____
_____
_____
_____
_____
_____

One awesome thing that
happened today was.......
_____
_____
_____
_____
_____
_____

**MY**
**HAPPINESS**
**SCALE**

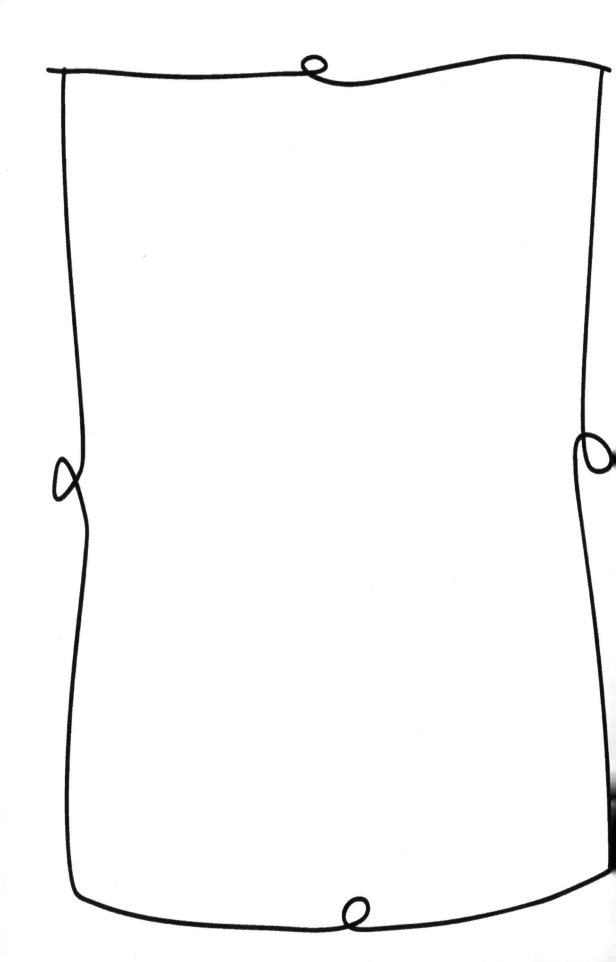

Today I am grateful for...........

_____
_____
_____
_____
_____
_____
_____
_____
_____
_____
_____
_____
_____

One awesome thing that
happened today was.......

_____
_____
_____
_____
_____
_____
_____
_____
_____

**MY HAPPINESS SCALE**

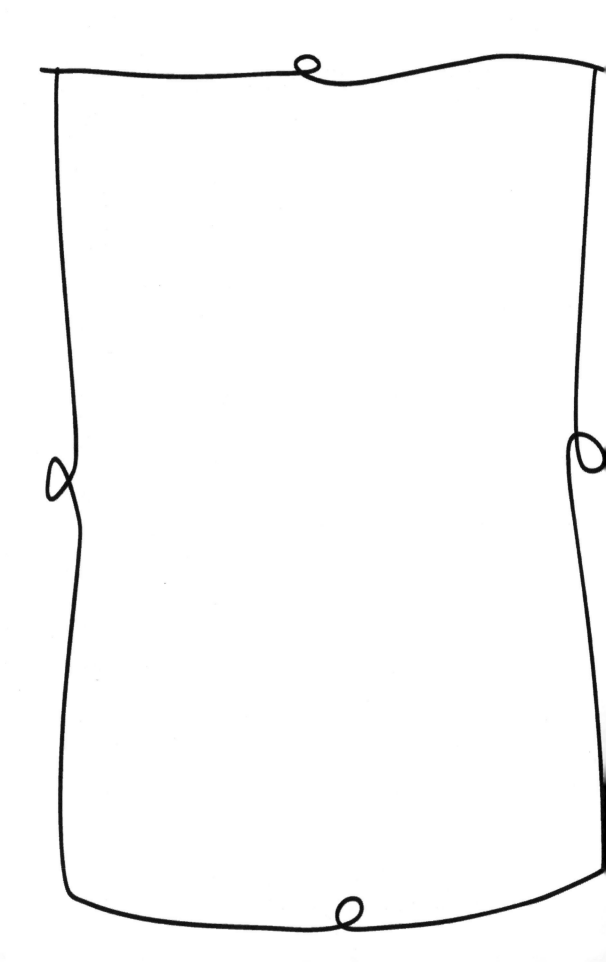

Today I am grateful for...........

One awesome thing that
happened today was.......

**MY HAPPINESS SCALE**

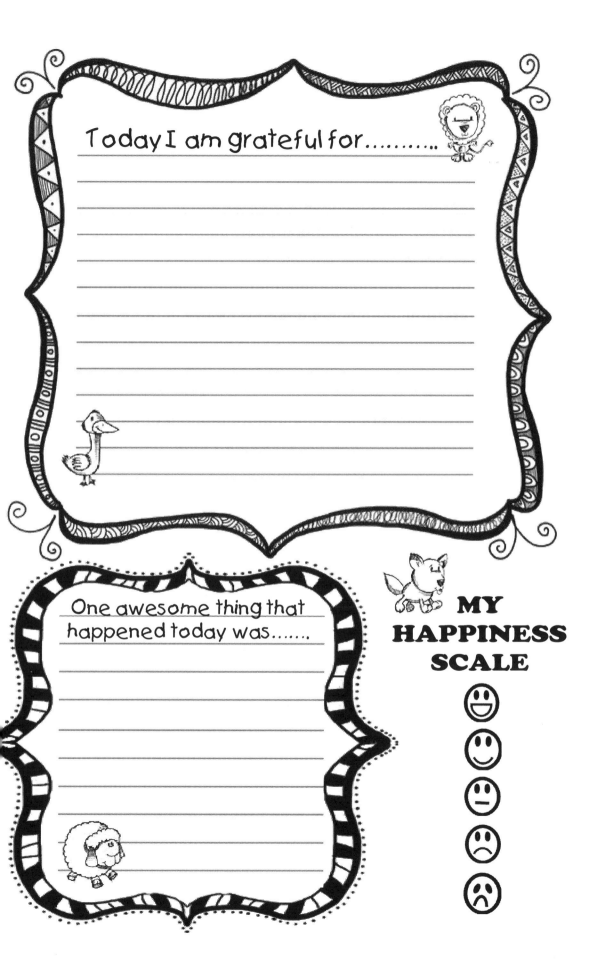

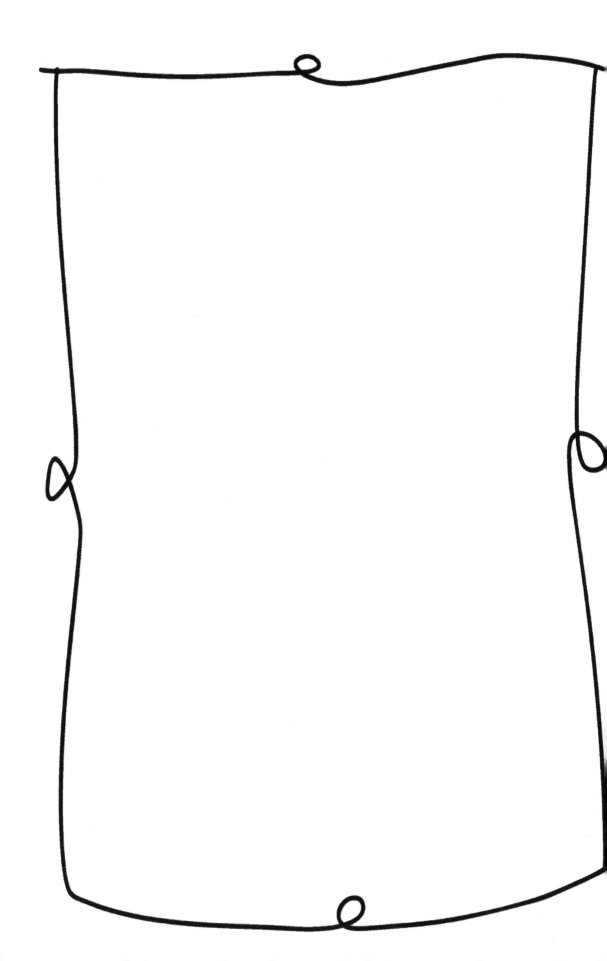

Today I am grateful for...........

One awesome thing that
happened today was.......

**MY**
**HAPPINESS**
**SCALE**

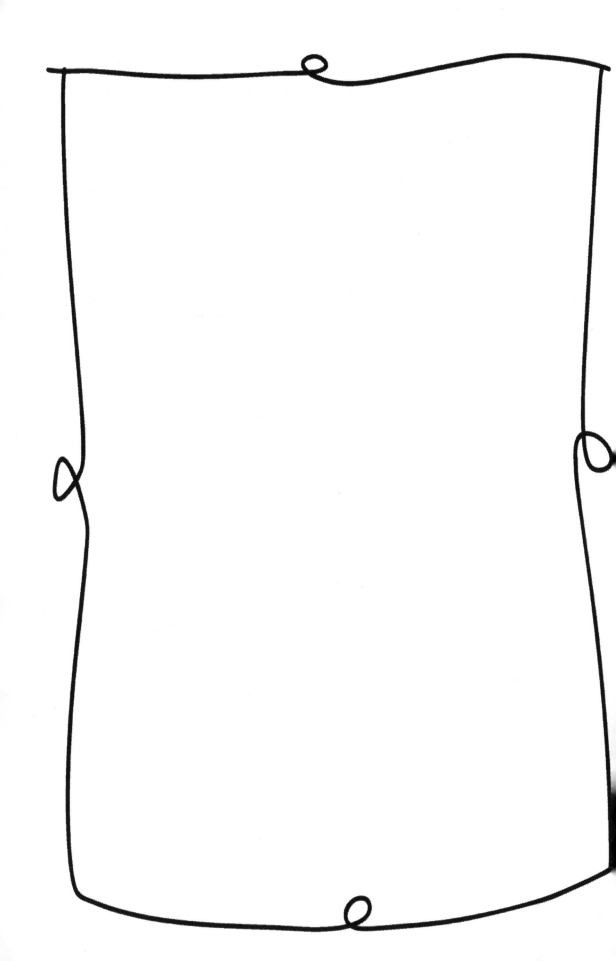

Today I am grateful for...........

_____
_____
_____
_____
_____
_____
_____
_____
_____
_____
_____
_____
_____

One awesome thing that
happened today was.......

_____
_____
_____
_____
_____
_____
_____
_____

**MY
HAPPINESS
SCALE**

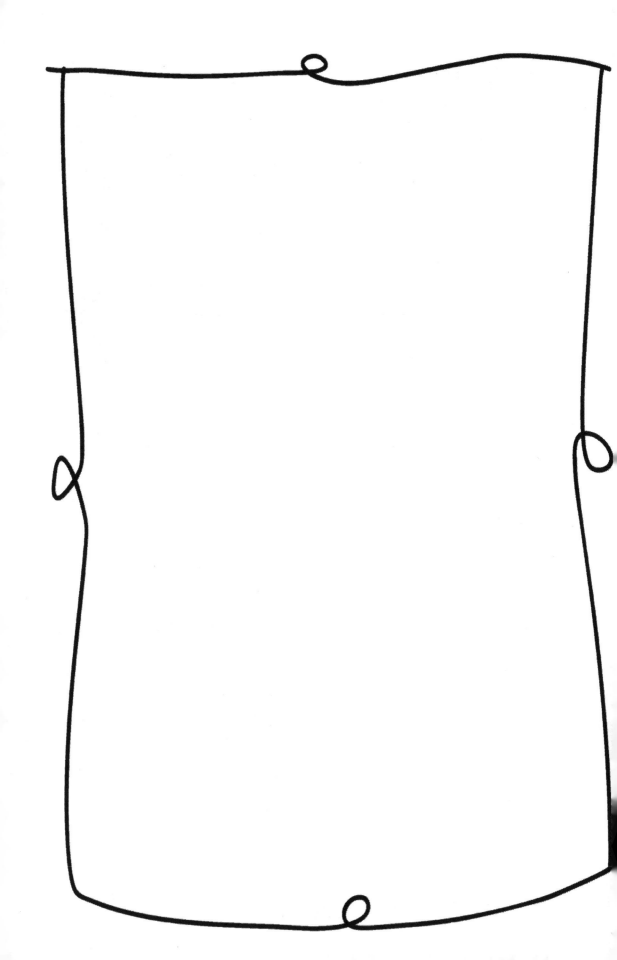

Today I am grateful for..........

One awesome thing that
happened today was.......

MY
HAPPINESS
SCALE

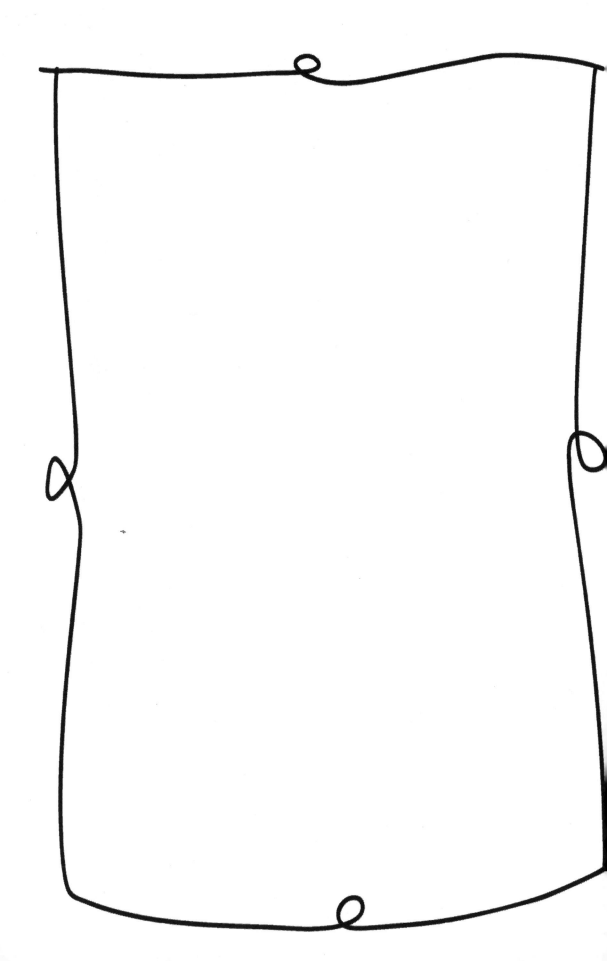

Today I am grateful for...........
_____
_____
_____
_____
_____
_____
_____
_____
_____
_____
_____
_____

One awesome thing that
happened today was.......
_____
_____
_____
_____
_____
_____
_____

**MY HAPPINESS SCALE**

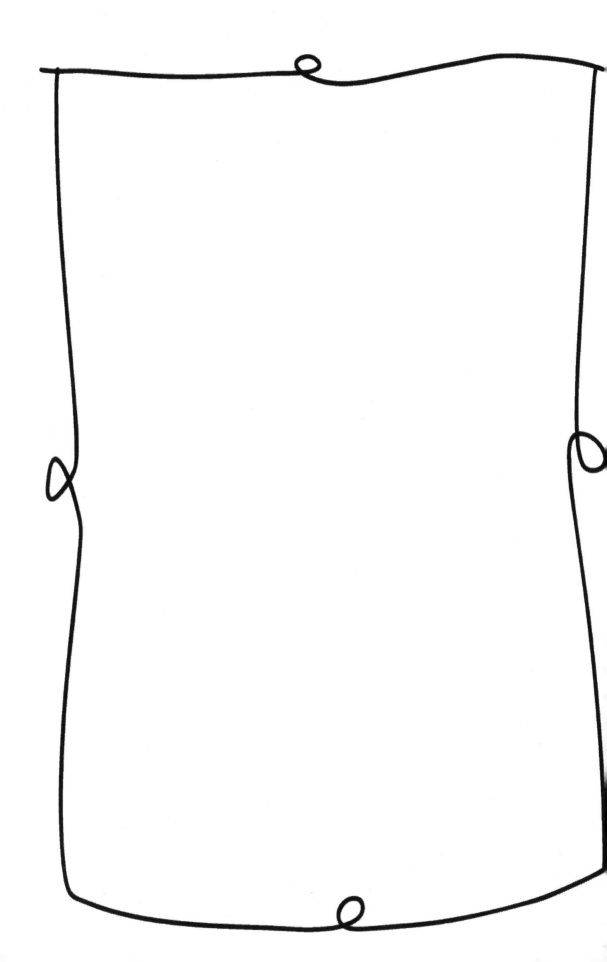

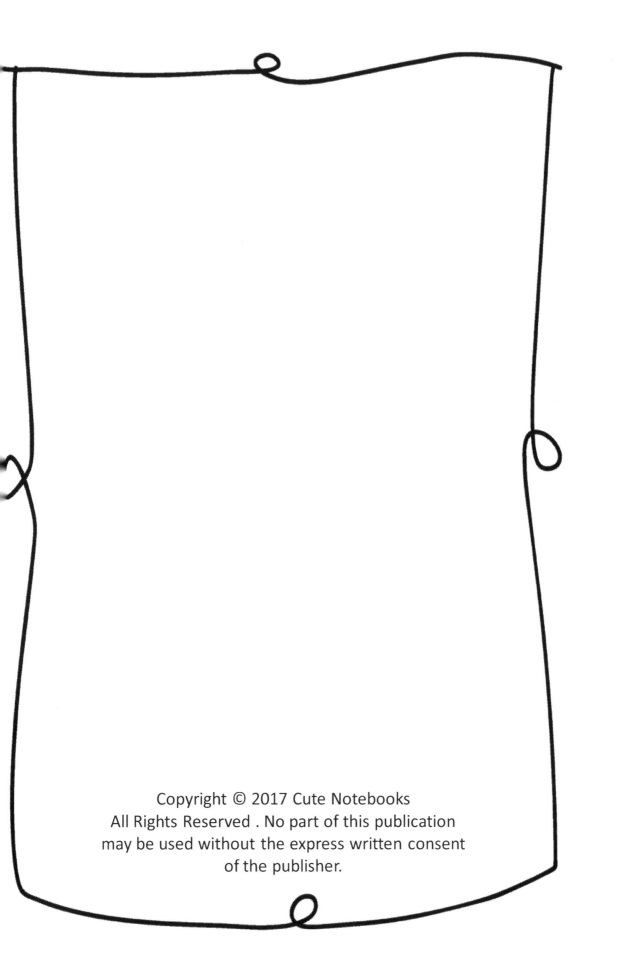

72608894R00064

Made in the USA
Middletown, DE
07 May 2018